A Woman's Hope

Brookie Peterson

BOOKCRAFT
Salt Lake City, Utah

Library of Congress Catalog Card Number: 91–70690

ISBN 0–88494–792–0

2nd Printing, 1991

Printed in the United States of America

For Burke

Press forward with a steadfastness
in Christ, having a perfect brightness
of hope.

—2 Nephi 31:20

Contents

I

A Woman's Challenge: Coping with
Frustrations of Everyday Living

II
A Woman's Words:
Communicating More Effectively
in Your Relationships

III
A Woman's Preparation:
Raising Your Level of Spirituality

Acknowledgments

Those whom I thank most for helping me with this book are my husband and daughters. My husband has encouraged me because he always shows respect not only for me but also for my mind. He thinks I can do anything, and that esteem from him convinces me to go ahead and try.

My daughters—who are, next to my husband, my most intimate friends—have taught me more lessons than I have taught them. My love and thanks go to them—Gayle Steele, Sherrie Decker, Robin Pedersen, Jana Staples, and Keri Nielsen—and to their husbands. Robin especially has given time and effort to the project and has provided many meaningful insights.

Appreciation goes to my good friend Susan Burningham, who has given reassurance and choice suggestions, besides eliminating at least one hundred "thats" from these pages. I express my thanks to other family members and friends who have offered ideas and comments.

I also express my gratitude to my Heavenly Father, whose guidance I have always sought and have felt abundantly many times.

Introduction: The Diversity of Women and Their Frustrations

Life today is complex, a puzzle of priorities, and this seems to be increasingly the case for modern women. Most of us are at times overwhelmed by all that we have to do. Gaining an understanding of the concerns other women have helps us put our own into perspective. Although we are dissimilar and struggle with different frustrations, we can gain universal answers and hope from the Savior's teachings.

Some years ago I accompanied my husband to a stake conference in southern Japan. Between meetings the stake president's wife served a lovely, light meal to the stake presidency, clerks, my husband, and me. Some other sisters helped. By their own choice the other wives did not sit down with us, so I was the only woman at the table. In spite of this difference, and the contrast in the food served, the meal seemed similar to many I had had in the United States. I imagined the sisters each bringing part of the meal and preparing it together in the kitchen at the meetinghouse.

When I pictured the Japanese sisters, I thought of the times I had driven in my car a short distance to my own ward building, carrying food to prepare meals. Then I realized they probably lived much far-

ther from their church building than I did from mine. I began to inquire: "Does Sister Tanaka live far away?" Through a translator I
learned it was indeed quite a distance. I asked if others had brought
part of the meal. I was told that the stake president's wife, Sister
Tanaka, had provided the food herself.

"Did it take long to get to the building?" and "Was the traffic
heavy?" were my next questions. The translator answered that traffic
is always congested in Japan. Then he explained that Sister Tanaka
had not driven to the church; she had carried the food on her bicycle
to the train depot and had ridden the train for about an hour, trans-
ferring twice to reach the church building.

It would be an understatement to say I was surprised to see how
different their way of preparing a church-served meal was from my
way.

I have met with endless surprises in discovering the diversity of
sisters in the Church around the world. Let me describe some other
examples.

In Singapore I visited in the home of a beautiful young woman, a
former Hindu, who joined the Church at age seventeen. She married
at eighteen—an arranged marriage—and for five long years she
didn't have the courage to tell her husband she was a Christian or to
ask if she might go to church. Her husband is Hindu, and they live in
a male-dominated society, but now he kindly allows her the privilege
of worshipping in her own way, of going to church on Sunday. She
and her husband live in a lovely, comfortable home.

The thatched huts of the Cuna Indians, who live off the coast of
Panama on the San Blas Islands, are very unlike the homes in Singapore. On these islands—which must be reached by small boats, complete with coconut shells for bailing out water—there are many
branches of the Church. The friendly Cuna sisters wear gold rings in
their noses for ornamental purposes, and they have never worn
shoes.

Just as different to us as the lives of the sisters in Singapore and
the San Blas Islands is the life of one of the first members of the
Church in the Philippines. She resides on an imposing estate that the
Japanese chose for their headquarters during World War II. It is huge,
with woodlands and a beachfront on the ocean. The estate includes
the swimming pool where the first nine baptisms, as well as many
later baptisms, in the Philippines took place.

I have described the diversity of sisters around the world because
I believe that you, whose dress and home may look similar to those of

others in your circle, are, in many unseen ways, almost as unlike your peers as the women described above are unlike you. That is to say, your hopes and challenges are unique. Our being in various seasons of life also makes for a tremendous dissimilarity among us.

I have several friends and acquaintances who are outstanding women—women who have coped with a variety of challenges and frustrations. As I have interviewed them about their hardships and hopes, I have gained a better understanding of women's frustrations. Surely some of these women are grappling with problems similar to yours.

I talked with Shelly, a young woman in the first season of her adulthood—a sophomore in college; Teri, married just over a year and very happy; Joan, in the crowded season of mothering, with children from toddlers to teens; Diane, divorced years ago while her children were young and now alone.

Sharon has not married, and though at times she feels lonely, she has adjusted to living by herself. Laurie courageously deals with multiple sclerosis. Helen and her husband long to have their own family, but the years are passing and there is less hope. June struggles to cope with the problems of being a single parent of young children. Peggy has two children who are severely handicapped.

Ellen is in the empty-nest season, with most of her children married and the last two in college. Alice was widowed two years ago. And finally, Caroline is in her aging season, the time when she is learning what enduring to the end means. I have learned from each of these sisters and hope to bring you some of their wisdom along with my own thoughts.

There is a universal need women have. Each woman, whatever her situation or season, has a need for a "brightness of hope." Nephi tells us, "Wherefore, ye must press forward with a steadfastness in Christ, having a perfect brightness of hope" (2 Nephi 31:20).

What unites us? It is our faith in the Savior and a tremendous desire to be obedient. It is also a long-range goal to become perfect, as our Savior has asked. I desire with all my heart that in reading the following pages you will gain some ideas you can use in facing your particular frustrations.

A woman's hope lies in meeting her challenges, building her relationships, and preparing herself spiritually. The sections of this book will address in detail these three vital areas.

In recognizing the uniqueness of each woman, I wish to celebrate it, for I believe Heavenly Father and the Savior want us to delight in

and enjoy it. No one exactly like you has been created the world over
—not now, nor in ages past. But in spite of our diversity, the same
principles of the gospel that help one will help another.

The gospel is broad and high and deep[1] enough to sustain each
distinct and different child of our heavenly parents. The plans to be
discussed in the three sections of this book—coping, communicating,
and increasing spirituality—are based on the gospel as taught to us
by Jesus Christ. In him we will find our hope and peace.

I

A Woman's Challenge: Coping with Frustrations of Everyday Living

1

Keep a Cheerful Attitude

Life is a series of problems. Jenkin Lloyd Jones observed: "Life is like an old-time rail journey—delays, sidetracks, smoke, dust, cinders, and jolts interspersed only occasionally by beautiful vistas and thrilling bursts of speed. The trick is to thank the Lord for letting you have the ride."[1] This quotation beautifully describes our life's passage amidst hardship and joy and suggests that we can be happy through it all.

The scriptures also encourage us to keep a cheerful attitude: "Let thy heart be of good cheer" (D&C 112:4); "A merry heart maketh a cheerful countenance" (Proverbs 15:13); "The hope of the righteous shall be gladness" (Proverbs 10:28).

Learning how other women have been cheerful and thankful in the face of enormous difficulties can motivate us to improve our own outlook.

Once, when my husband and I were spending a few days in the mission home in the Dominican Republic, I met a young woman about age twenty-four. She and her husband, a medical student, were from Utah. They had a little boy who was probably nine or ten months old. I asked her, "What has been the hardest thing for you to adjust to since coming to the island?" She told me that at first she had been excited to travel and anxious to have new experiences, but the culture shock was great and gradually she became discouraged. As her feelings of dislike for her new surroundings grew, she became quite unhappy.

Perhaps the hardest time came one day when she was preparing to wash a bucket of diapers. To her dismay she found that the lid had been left slightly ajar and the diapers were covered with maggots. If she had been at home she would have burned them or dug a hole and buried them, but in the Dominican Republic she simply had to clean them. It wasn't possible to get any more.

By the time she went home for Christmas, she could hardly have been more depressed. Her mother soon recognized the daughter's feelings. She told her daughter that she alone could decide whether her experience would be happy or miserable during the next four years. "You can 'bloom where you're planted' or spend the time longing for your husband's graduation so you can return home—it will be your decision," her mother emphasized.

The young wife had a clear understanding of her mother's words and could imagine how miserable it would be to feel unhappy the whole time she was away from home. She decided that wasn't what she wanted and was able to change her whole attitude. Through her discussion with her mother (her mother being someone she trusted) as well as through logic, she gained the strength to know she could not only tolerate but enjoy a place and a people who were so significantly different. She told me that since the time of her return to Dominica she had felt peaceful and interested in her surroundings. Though conditions had not improved, she was now in charge and involved in making her life joyful.

I wonder if you have heard about Caroline Eyring, Sister Camilla Kimball's mother, who was a lifetime optimist. She must have lived by the scripture, "A merry heart doeth good like a medicine" (Proverbs 17:22). Another of her daughters, Caroline Miner, tells us: "To mother . . . the small town of Pima, Arizona, in which we lived was the most wonderful town in the whole world." (May I remind you that she went there in the days of no air conditioning.) Her daughter continues:

> She marveled at the sunrises and sunsets, at the weeds in bloom, at the smoothness of the cacti where there were no

thorns. Most of all, she loved "the dear hearts and gentle people." Every play she saw, every lecture she heard, every song was simply heavenly. She was without guile and without criticism. She made life a bluebird of paradise, even though we were refugees from old Mexico and were struggling to get enough work to keep food in our mouths. The song in her heart made the difference.[2]

A song on our lips can make a difference also. Whenever I'm happy I sing; whenever I'm sad I also sing. When things are on an even keel I may be silent. In times of strain or stress, however, the songs I sing can help bring the happy feelings back. We may not all have cacti in our lives, but many of us have thorns. When I hear about Sister Eyring it inspires me to try harder to see the beauty amidst my thorns.

Sister Eyring's daughter Caroline, a former Utah Mother of the Year, said that two tenets have helped her maintain a wholesome, happy attitude: "(1) It isn't what happens to you but how you take what happens that makes all the difference, and (2) make the most of all that comes and the least of all that goes."[3]

Throughout her life my own mother constantly focused on her blessings. She had an awareness of and felt gratitude for all good things, no matter how common. That attitude helped her block out the heartaches. When she experienced tribulation, her philosophy was to look forward, as soon as possible, not back. Her concentration was on the future. It helped her to have a habitually happy outlook.

Mother passed away a few years ago. She had a debilitating disease for the last fifteen years of her life. During her final two months she didn't have the strength to swallow and was fed through a tube. Because of weakness she could say no more than three audible words. It was necessary for her to have an oxygen mask, and she couldn't turn herself at all in her bed. Her feet had to be padded because the skin was so fragile and sore. A miserable, convulsive cough tormented her. Most of the time her mind was alert. After doing all we could to make her comfortable we would ask, "Are you all right, Mother?" In spite of her suffering she never answered anything but a simple, "Yes," accompanied by a slight, affirmative nod. In her time of trouble she maintained the optimistic attitude of a lifetime.

The ways we can keep a cheerful attitude sometimes seem so simple that we don't implement them but instead end up, to borrow a phrase from Jacob, "looking beyond the mark" (Jacob 4:14). One of the first things we can do is discuss frustrations with someone we trust. Often through discussion we come to a recognition of our problems and find answers in our own statements. It is important to keep in mind that it is normal to feel discouraged and depressed at times. As we suffer we learn, and as time heals we can reach for a brighter day. Try singing when you're happy and singing when you're blue, until you make a habit of it.

Some kinds of despondency require medical help, but for overcoming temporary unhappiness good health habits of rest, exercise, and physical tasks are solutions women all know about but often neglect. When you decide you can feel happier, resolve not to look back; instead look to the future and concentrate on the good things. Search for the beauties of your life and you will become blind to the thorns.

2

Set Priorities and Simplify, Simplify!

I have learned that each woman who is at peace concerning her activities and feels she is spending her time in the most productive way has spent some effort with setting priorities. Such efforts are usually not easy. "Bruce C. Hafen . . . related the suppressed frustration of an overworked, somewhat harassed young mother who, when advised to 'just be sure you put the Lord's work first,' blurted out in near desperation, 'But what if it is *all* the Lord's work?' "[1]

We simplify our lives when we set eternal priorities as our guides. Gospel principles will help us identify what choices fit into eternal priorities. Measuring by those guidelines we can overcome some of the guilt feelings that sometimes arise when we can't do everything we would like to do. Enduring to the end is one of the critical eternal priorities.

Choices and Talents

I'd like to introduce to you Dr. Anne Osborn Poelman, a convert who joined the Church during her university years. She is an emi-

nent neuroradiologist and has served on the Relief Society General
Board. Tall and striking in looks, she is one of the most interesting,
captivating women I know. In the medical profession she has enjoyed
international acclaim. Until her mid-thirties she was unmarried, but
then she married a widowed General Authority.

In the book *Joy* she observes:

> Most choices we face are . . . not between right and wrong but
> between right and right. Few of us have to choose between
> holding family home evening and robbing a bank. More often
> the most difficult decisions are between equally attractive, wor-
> thy activities. . . . Should we get in that long overdue temple
> session or take the children on an outing?[2]

We need to learn not to feel guilty because we are unable to do two
good things at the same time.

While Dr. Osborn was still unmarried, one evening she invited
my husband and me to her home for dinner. There were just the
three of us. It was evident that though she lived alone she was an accomplished homemaker with gourmet-cooking skills and artistic
home-decorating accomplishments. As we sat at the table after a
pleasant and delicious meal we spoke of feelings close to our hearts. I
said, "Anne, I have always wondered if I could have learned to be a
doctor"—for being an internist always appealed to me and seemed to
fit with some of the skills I have. She replied thoughtfully, "Brookie, I
have always wondered if I could have learned to be a wife and
mother."

A year or two later, as she knelt at an altar in the Salt Lake
Temple, I remembered her remark. I thought of it again that evening
at a garden reception as she stood, a beautiful woman in softly
sculptured white satin, beside her new husband, a tall, handsome,
kind man, and received the love and best wishes of many friends.

On an earlier occasion, speculating about a time when she might
have children, she had reflected, "My children will probably never
appear in the ward Christmas program wearing stunning outfits I
carefully crafted for them. I've learned to sew people but not clothes!
While I can and do admire the talent of those who have, I won't feel
guilty about clothing family in 'store-bought' dresses."[3]

You may be thinking, "Well, if I could sew people, I wouldn't
worry about making dresses!" But it doesn't matter which valued

traits you possess or how many talents you have been blessed with. Our responsibility is to make the best use of our time and to be diligent in increasing our talents. We do not have to be the best or achieve the most. The Lord appreciates and rewards careful, prudent effort.

In Every Season, Simplify!

Life is filled with important activities, so we must simplify, simplify. Some worthy goals will have to take a minor position at certain seasons of our lives. The answer is to pick and choose—to say no sometimes in order to keep moderation and balance in our lives. I was once talking to a friend who is a well-known speaker. She said she would be giving twenty-two talks during the month of March, sometimes two per day. Someone asked, "Do you ever say no?" She grinned widely and said, "Maybe I'll have to learn to do that."

If you can't say no but you believe you should, you could say, "Let me think about it." Then you will have time to consider the request and won't be drawn into undertakings which are not among your top priorities and which you haven't the strength to perform.

Many of you may solve a problem by hiring some secretarial or household help. There is nothing wrong with paying a high school girl to address Christmas cards or help do the cleaning, or with securing the services of an older person for such work. When we had three young children—our oldest being seven years old—I was president of the Young Women. Once a week, for four hours, our fourteen-year-old neighbor from across the street came over to fold clothes, straighten the children's drawers, and wash the floors. What a lift it gave me! It cost only about double what baby-sitting does—really a relatively small amount—and she loved having the job. That much help made a world of difference.

Grandmothers who don't have the time or strength to baby-sit grandchildren as much as they would like to could, perhaps, help the young parents pay for a competent sitter from time to time. This would solve two problems and be much appreciated.

Since we can't do everything we would like to do—there is neither time nor strength—we must be creative. After her divorce Diane, a single parent, found that she couldn't be everywhere she wanted to be, though she tried. She struggled to find the time to support her children in their activities. A solution came as she found she could go to part of a concert and then walk in for the last thirty minutes of a football game. She said she made eye contact with her children at each event so that they knew she had arrived.

Perhaps you can save time by studying the little book *One Minute Mother.*[4] This book shows how lectures to your children can be condensed to the length of one minute. The children will be grateful for your conciseness, and you will conserve time and energy. Brevity is sometimes a true virtue. Simplifying takes some creative thinking, but often there are easier yet productive ways to do things. I have a tendency to be a perfectionist, but my husband tells me to remember that I'm not always building a Swiss watch and that some things do not merit the time it would take to do them perfectly.

Overcoming Guilt Feelings

There are some responsibilities that women often have guilt feelings about. I mean things like genealogy, journals, life histories, and so forth. If you have a true desire to perfect yourself in God-given directives the time will come when you can make that emphasis, because you will move into another season of life. Remember, "To every thing there is a season, and a time to every purpose under the heaven: . . . a time to get, and a time to lose; a time to keep, and a time to cast away" (Ecclesiastes 3:1, 6).

Elder Dallin H. Oaks gives us some words of comfort concerning our responsibility to help accomplish the mission of the Church in its three dimensions. Referring particularly to work for the dead, he points out that "there are many tasks to be performed, and . . . all members should participate by prayerfully selecting those ways that fit their personal circumstances at a particular time." He goes on to say:

> Some members may feel guilty about not furthering the mission of the Church when they are actually doing so. This kind of guilt comes not from insufficient efforts, but from insufficient vision. For example, a mother with several young children may be furthering the mission of the Church most profoundly in all three of its dimensions in her own home when she helps her children to prepare for missions, when she

teaches them to revere the temple and prepare to make covenants there, and when she shows them how to strive for perfection in their personal lives.[5]

King Benjamin helps us to judge how well we are handling our stewardships: "And see that all these things are done in wisdom and order; for it is not requisite that a man should run faster than he has strength. And again, it is expedient that he should be diligent, that thereby he might win the prize; therefore, all things must be done in order." (Mosiah 4:27.) That is, we are not required to run faster than we have strength, but at the same time we are urged to be diligent. This balance will be a protection.

One of the mothers I interviewed, her children now grown, told me, "It almost seems that this is my time to study the scriptures more intensely. At last I also write in my journal. I even read for fun." She does all this, though she works full-time in the nursing profession.

Stressing Eternal Priorities

Let your priorities be of *eternal* value. To a young mother with small children it is a temptation to put her children ahead of her husband, because their needs are so immediate and insistent. The demands from teenagers sometimes make a mother almost frantic because of their claims on her time. While it is essential that a couple work together for their children (and I think a woman should ask for the father's help perhaps more often in some cases), it is of eternal importance that the wife put her husband at the head of her list—and vice versa.

Make your husband your closest friend. Put him above a Church calling or any other interest or person, including your children. At the end of your life you will know that this was right and you will be thankful you did it. It is in the children's best interest as well; it is far better for them to know that their parents are first in one another's lives than to have your help on a school project or your company at certain times.

This focus on our husbands is to be kept in balance, of course. Sometimes we face difficult choices and we make mistakes, but if we know the principle of "husband first" we will do what is best more often.

I would like to quote from a letter written by a young woman to the columnist Ann Landers. Her message is so timeless that it has been reprinted upon request more than once. (It was written in the day when most women stayed at home.) The young woman was commenting about a previous letter, written by a wife who complained about all the extra work that having a husband caused her. The first writer had grumbled that she had to prepare his meals, put up with his relatives, run his errands, keep his house in order, take care of him when he was sick, and on and on. The second writer responded:

> My husband is a laborer. He leaves the house at 7 a.m. and puts in a long hard day's work. If he can get overtime he grabs it. When he comes home at night he paints the house, fixes whatever needs it (and something always does), keeps our car running, and helps with the kids. At the end of the week he hands me his paycheck and apologizes because it isn't more.
>
> He never complains when I give him ground meat in 11 different forms. At night when he puts his arms around me and pulls me close I feel that whatever I've done for him during the day wasn't enough.
>
> Love and marriage are like a circle. The more you do for a man the more he loves you. The more he loves you the more he tries to do for you. The more he tries to do for you the more you love him. And so it goes. It's so simple. Why don't more people figure it out?

The answer from Ann Landers is also touching: "I've read nearly a million letters, but yours got to me as few have. The next time you fix ground meat in one of those 11 forms, please know you are the envy of thousands of women who will be dining on filet mignon."

Enduring

Enduring to the end is another critical priority. Perhaps when a woman is older she is tempted to say, "I have worked hard in the Church for more than fifty years; I am due for a rest now. Let the younger women in the ward teach the classes in Relief Society, take the teenagers to camp, and sing with the Primary children. I've had my turn." But, if we have adequate health, should our efforts in the Church ever cease? I think they should continue for our whole lifetime.

When our youngest daughter was seventeen she went to camp and came home having had a much better time than she had expected to. (She was never a camper!) She startled her father when she said, "Dad, I've found out there's just no excuse for you to act as old as you do! Sister Hogan went to camp with us. She went on all the hikes and roasted marshmallows with us, and she even won the canoe race. You know very well she's three years older than you are!" We may not all be Sister Hogans, but we can remain willing and helpful.

When I was a temple matron, almost every week I had the privilege of visiting with Sister Camilla Kimball. She would come to the temple, go on a session in a wheelchair, and then I would have the choice opportunity of having her and her daughter as my guests for lunch. Each time I would invite a few others to eat with us. Some of these, because of personal trials, needed a spiritual uplift, and we always received one by being with her.

I loved to hear her tell about visiting teaching. In answer to the question, "Sister Kimball, are you still a visiting teacher?" she enthusiastically replied, "Oh yes, it is one of my favorite things to do." When asked, "How many women's homes do you go to?" she answered, "I have four sisters to teach. Each one is a young mother with little children. I love to see the children and talk to the mothers. It's one of the highlights of my month!" Sister Kimball was ninety-one at the time, and she often told me that she never knew it would be so hard to endure to the end. But every week at the temple it was evident that she was doing it beautifully.

Measuring our activities and choices by eternal priorities helps us simplify our lives. We need to remember that we are not required to accomplish all things in each season but rather to make the best choices for ourselves as individuals in whatever season we are in, thus allowing ourselves to be at peace.

3

Take Time for a Halcyon Day

I once heard a story about a former Relief Society president,[1] a story that had a great impact on me. You may enjoy hearing it, because it tells of one way to nurture yourself that will renew your vitality and zest. This sister was a Relief Society president before the block meeting program was introduced, and her ward's monthly homemaking meeting was carefully planned for Tuesday morning. On Tuesday the breakfast tasks were humming along when her six-year-old son came out of his room. His eyes were swollen and obviously needed medical attention. Sighing, she said, "Whatever else I do today, I must take him to the doctor."

After arriving at the doctor's office she was kept waiting for some time. Leafing through a magazine she saw a one-page story and thought, "I'll probably be here long enough to read that." The story was entitled "The Halcyon Day." She thought, "Now, I've seen that word before." (Later, at home, she looked it up and learned that *halcyon* means "tranquil, happy, peaceful, golden."[2])

The magazine story was about a little boy. One morning he got up, got dressed, took his lunch, and started his walk to school. He walked the two blocks to the school and kept right on walking past the building! In another four blocks he reached the shore of a lake that was near the little town. (The story was written in that long ago day when it was safe for little boys to walk around little towns alone.)

The sand on the lake's shore was already soft and warm. He put down his lunch, took off his shoes, and wiggled his toes in the sand. He made a sand castle. When the sun got warmer he took off his shirt; when he got hungry he ate his lunch. He saw a stick, made a fishing pole, and went fishing. He didn't catch any fish, but he went fishing. At the end of the school day he put his shirt back on, picked up his lunch pail, and walked back home.

With that, the story concluded. There was no moralizing. That was the end. When the Relief Society president finished reading the story that day in the doctor's office, she felt tears rolling down her face. She hoped the others in the waiting room would think she was one of the patients, that her eyes were watering for that reason. The real reason why she felt so sad was that she thought, "I never have a day like that."

She finally got to the homemaking meeting, which went well, but later when she went home she put a big red *H* on a particular date on her calendar. The children asked what it was for, but she didn't tell them. When her "Halcyon Day" came she got her husband off to work and the children off to school, then she put bubbles in the tub and had a lovely, relaxing bath.

There was a new mall opening. After dressing she went there and browsed through the bookstore. Thumbing through a lot of books that looked interesting, she bought a paperback. Next she visited a dress shop, where she looked around and tried on some blouses but didn't buy anything. She had a wonderfully happy Halcyon Day and felt much more like cherishing her family because she had spent a little time nurturing herself.

Now she puts a red *H* on her calendar three or four times a year; sometimes it's on a weekend and she and her husband go somewhere together. One of her Halcyon Days she had spent skiing; another, reading; one had been spent in the temple.

I think she had a good idea, and I don't think it was a selfish one. Because of the season you're now in, some of you couldn't schedule an entire day for yourself, but you *could* find an hour or maybe a half day. Try it—it will renew you.

I recall that a Church leader once said, in effect, "You will have bad days, days you can't do anything about; so when you have one of them, just sit back and enjoy it!"

When you need a respite, a lift on a bad day, or a relief from stress, you might try going to a place where you can feel and be close to the beauty of woodland, flowers, or seascape. Nature has a great healing calm to impart. Take a walk or a drive, sit in your yard or a park and observe the outdoor world of minute creatures around you, or absorb the magnificence of the gold-red sun going down in the quiet of the evening.

You might also try doing something different, no matter how minor. Make a change—new ways always intrigue and refresh us. Here are a few ideas:

—Rearrange the furniture in your bedroom. (Get help if you have a bad back.)
—Even if you have to go grocery shopping, do it in a new way—go with a friend or to a different market, or go alone instead of with the children.
—Go out for lunch. If you usually eat out, bring a lunch from home or eat lunch at a new little place.
—Stop at the perfume counter; try a new scent and ask for a perfume sample.
—Take a child to the playground. Have a little picnic afterwards.
—Buy a new kind of juice or treat yourself to fresh pineapple or tender asparagus.
—Take a favorite paperback with you on a visit to a friend and leave the book with her.
—Make arrangements so that you can take a nap or a relaxing bubble bath.
—Take a child with you and drive to a creek; you and the child throw rocks in the creek.[3]

These may not be activities that appeal to you, but perhaps reading the preceding list can get you thinking creatively about ways you can add something different and pleasing to your life, even if only for an hour. If you can learn to nurture yourself, you will increase your capacity to care for others. Then you and those you love will be more content.

4

Value Yourself

You may have heard some of the girls in the Young Women program recite their values. They say, among other things, "I am of infinite worth with my own divine mission which I will strive to fulfill." As women we should each come to realize that being a daughter of God gives us value. Unfortunately, while we accept this truth for everyone else, we often do not recognize it for ourselves.

As each new season of our lives unfolds we develop significant attributes, but often we don't give ourselves enough credit for this progress. We don't think of these qualities as talents. We, as well as others, often place too much emphasis on valuing ourselves because of outward accomplishments. But we should come to realize that our homespun traits that bless others are of great worth and consequence.

Three women in my neighborhood come to mind. Undoubtedly you have the same types of women among your friends. One of them is an expert at making pies. She has used her talent in countless ways and has taught many how to make pies quickly and deliciously. Numerous families have seen ordinary days become special ones as other

women, following this good sister's simple directions, have surprised
their loved ones with a pie for dinner. Often girls or boys have felt
loved when this sister has presented them with a pie on a festive occasion.

Another woman is talented at making her husband feel loved.
When she shares some of her ideas with us we all listen; we know
they are unique and we prize them.

The third woman is probably unaware of how much happiness
she gives. We love to be around her because she is so sensitive to our
needs that she makes us *value* ourselves; we go away from a visit with
her feeling uplifted, able to conquer new problems, and aware that
perhaps we are doing well with some of the old ones. These three examples help us to realize that it isn't only in the performing arts or in
athletics that there is meaningful achievement.[1]

We need to work hard to eliminate the guilt which we always
manage to feel when we compare ourselves with others. Elder Russell
M. Nelson has said that a woman "could become discouraged, especially if comparing herself unrealistically to others or focusing on
what she is to do instead of what she is to be."[2] Making comparisons
between ourselves and others is nonproductive. Judging from the par-
able of the talents, I don't believe that our Heavenly Father compares
his children one with another. Rather, he judges us on how well we
have developed the unique set of talents and abilities he has blessed
us with. We can determine progress through comparing ourselves to
what we were like a month ago, a year ago, or a decade ago. If we are
headed upwards, we are doing well.

We can make progress through striving for personal improvement. My friend who works in personnel at the Church Office Building told me of a widow who came in to apply for work. Her husband
had been dead for three years. During all that time she had stayed at
home and made keeping her home and yard her only occupation;
when the wind blew a leaf off the tree, she went out and picked it up.
She was afraid to try anything new, and she was unhappy and terribly lonely.

Then she began working at the Church Office Building, doing
some volunteer work for a half day each week. Gradually she became
very useful. Those in charge asked if she would take part-time work.
She did, and saved the money. Recently she called and invited my
friend to attend her mission farewell. My friend told me she saw a
confident woman, not the shy, lonely one she had first met.

Few know the devastating despair that some divorcées feel. A friend told me that she felt she had followed gospel guidelines in her marriage and could scarcely believe it when she was faced with a divorce. She described some heartrending situations. One day she found her seven-year-old boy lying under his bed, sobbing. All he could say was, "I just want my daddy to come home." She said her situation was so terrible and she thought herself such a failure that one weekend she reached the point of deciding to take her life.

The children were safely gone for the day. But just at the moment of decision the ten-year-old girl returned home. "When I looked into her face, I remembered a forgotten promise I had made to her after the divorce," the mother recalled. "I had said, 'Julie, I will never leave you.' At the time of that thought I resolved to keep my promise. From that moment I went up."

But it wasn't a smooth path; the process that helped her most was learning to stop thinking, "Why? Why?" and forcing herself to reflect on good experiences and successes with her children, in her employment, and in her own spiritual growth. She evidently had a lot of success, because her three children, who all married in the temple, are some of the finest young people I have ever met.

In learning to value ourselves it is important to concentrate on our positive accomplishments. We should remember to put our mistakes and failures out of our minds after we have learned the lessons they teach, and we should concentrate on giving ourselves credit for the good things we are doing. We need to reflect on every success, major or minor, frequently.

II

*A Woman's Words:
Communicating More Effectively
in Your Relationships*

5

How Vital Is
Communication?

A little story may help us see the need for more clarity and sensitivity in family communication:

> Matthew, my 3½-year-old son, was eating an apple in the back seat of the car, when he asked, "Daddy, why is my apple turning brown?"
>
> "Because," I explained, "after you ate the skin off, the meat of the apple came into contact with the air which caused it to oxidize thus changing its molecular structure and turning it into a different color." There was a long silence. Then Matthew asked softly, "Daddy, are you talking to me?"[1]

Many times I have questioned, What can be done to improve family relationships, enjoyment of life, adjustment to children, and happiness of husband and wife during their crowded years, as well as after they once more become a "couple" family? Surprisingly there is an answer which can help us improve in each of these areas. The answer is one of the most important but often most neglected resources to improve families—accurate and comprehensive communication.

It has been only since the 1970s that professional counselors have begun to realize that communication is at the heart of all our associations. There is much yet to learn about its potential influence for good in family life and friendships. From my observation of people and their problems, I believe one of the most crucial needs in all relationships is better understanding of communication skills.

In speaking of communication in families we automatically include people beyond the immediate family circle. Single people, as well as the rest of us, will use these skills in many other "family associations." Here Carolyn Rasmus explains some meanings of the word *family* that apply to everyone, including those who are single:

> We all have and are a part of a family. These are "families of orientation." They include our "genealogy families"—our parents and siblings, as well as our extended family of grandparents, aunts, uncles, nieces, nephews, and cousins; our "gospel families"—members of the Church who share common eternal goals and show Christlike love to those around them; and our "neighborhood families," who, because they live closer to us than anyone else, can be the first to whom we turn when we need help, friendship, or just a kind word.[2]

Think how peaceable your home and neighborhood would be if every person, when angry, could learn to make noninsulting statements and cordial requests. Too often instead of courtesy there are confrontations, threats, and name-calling. But we can make an effort to be courteous and kind when dealing with others.

For example, when a thirteen-year-old grandson stays overnight, you can be pretty sure that in the morning the bathroom will have a towel wadded on the floor or counter, an unlidded shampoo bottle tipped over, and a bar of soap waiting underfoot to cause a disaster in the shower. Don't look at the mess, make no demands, utter no insults, but simply appeal, "Cameron, will you leave the bathroom in a way that I can't tell you were there?" Back he will go in a good humor and put it in order.

Courteous and pleasant requests work as well with children as with grandchildren. Beware of compelling commands. Elder Russell M. Nelson recalls an incident that occurred when his youngest daughter was about four years old:

I came home from work one night to find my sweetheart very weary from a full day with nine children underfoot. My day had been heavy also, but I offered to get the children ready for bed. I began to give the orders to our little four-year-old daughter: take your clothes off, hang them up, brush your teeth, put on your pajamas, say your prayers, and so forth, commanding in a manner befitting a tough sergeant in the army. Suddenly she cocked her head to one side, looked at me with wistful eyes, and said, "Daddy, do you own me?"

Then I realized that I was using coercive methods on this sweet spirit, and that to rule children by command or force is the technique of Satan, not of the Savior. She taught me this important lesson. We don't own our children; we only have them for a brief season. As parents, it is our privilege to love them, to lead them, and then to let them go. The Lord said, "I have commanded you to bring up your children in light and truth" (D&C 93:40). This we have tried to do.[3]

When we learn to be skilled communicators we can be as pleasant as Ronald Reagan while being as effectual as Eleanor Roosevelt.

There are many relationships, both inside and outside of the family, that are impacted by our expertise as clear communicators. Effective communication is a skill which can be learned. Two of the most important steps are simply awareness and practice.

In the next chapters the vital nature of good communication will become as apparent as the need for it in the following domestic scene:

One morning a woman said to her husband as he was leaving for work, "I'll bet you don't know what day this is."

"Of course I know what day this is," he replied resentfully. And with that he left for the office.

Later that morning a knock came at the door, and the woman was delighted to find that it was a delivery for her — a dozen red roses. A big box of gourmet chocolates arrived in the afternoon, and towards evening the local jewelry store delivered a beautiful pearl necklace.

Excitedly the woman awaited her husband's return home. When he finally arrived she hugged him and exclaimed, "Oh, sweetheart, first the roses, then the chocolates, and then the necklace — I can't remember when I have had such a perfectly wonderful Groundhog Day!"

6

Self-Image and
Communication

"You never do anything right!"

"You're not as pretty as your sister."

"You are not worthy to ask for blessings, because you make so many foolish mistakes."

"How can you be so stupid?"

"You're not as sharp as your parents."

These would be devastating remarks to hear from anyone, no matter the level of your self-esteem! Now suppose they were worded this way:

"I never do anything right!"

"I'm not as pretty as Bette."

"I'm not worthy to ask for blessings in my prayers; I make too many dumb mistakes."

"How could I do anything so brainless?"

"I don't have as much on the ball as Mom and Dad."

They are still desolating observations whether you hear them from someone else or from yourself. We are just as credible a source of information as our friends or enemies are. Thus self-criticism can be extremely destructive. We can't change what others say about us, but we can change what *we* say, and eventually what we think, about ourselves.

The way a woman feels about herself will determine the way she presents herself; that is, her self-image will lead her to use either generally optimistic or generally pessimistic inflections and language. Thus our self-image influences the messages we send to others. Also it serves as a filter through which messages we receive from others must pass. To a large extent we judge ourselves according to the reactions and responses of those around us. In many ways self-concept governs communication, and communication promotes or limits a person's success.

I once heard a doctor of psychology explain that almost every problem he had been called upon to help correct had at its core a person's lack of self-esteem. We need only to think of some of the problems people face and their causes to realize the truth of what he said.

Does a fourteen-year-old who is having a successful day and is feeling good about herself lash out at her parents or siblings? If someone has confidence in herself, has she any need to make herself feel more accepted by using drugs? Does a person who is pleased with himself turn to alcohol or child abuse?

People who have confidence in their own worth are usually successful and happy in a multitude of ways. Those who doubt their value have difficulties in almost every phase of life—they will usually have trouble making financial, social, and spiritual adjustments.

I know a certain man who held a position of leadership in the Church, and I often heard him say, "I don't know why they would choose me; I'm not clever or a student of the scriptures, and I'm a timid, second-rate speaker." He would talk himself down until those over whom he presided also wondered why he was chosen. Every time this man spoke of himself in a critical way, his self-esteem was lowered another notch. Through the help of some friends he came to realize what he was doing, and he learned to stop the self-disparagement before it left his lips. It was even more difficult for him to learn to squelch such thoughts when they entered his mind. But now his family hears him say, "I know I have contributions to make; I know that when I try to live the Lord's commandments he will magnify me."

Just as this man learned to recognize his desirable qualities as well

as his undesirable ones, you can become more objective about yourself if you will honestly seek to identify the positive characteristics
and abilities you have and capitalize on them by developing them.

It is difficult to separate yourself from your actions. Often you determine your worth or inconsequence through judgment of your behavior. But you need to believe you are of value no matter what your
actions may be. You can always improve your conduct if you believe
in your abilities. Doubting that you have the power to change can be
a great obstacle, but you can overcome it. One important way is
through what is known as self-talk.

Self-Talk

Most of us have learned to say positive, uplifting things about our
children and our spouses and to praise the good in others. We over-
look their mistakes and try to help them by always finding their best
features. Perhaps we have not learned to do this with ourselves, but
rather we constantly think negatively and reproachfully of our own
behavior. It is possible to unlearn this harmful habit and change from
self-criticism to self-approval.

You may have censured yourself for so long that you are unfair.
You know what you do well, but you may think, "It's true I did that
in a competent, efficient manner, but it's not important." Or you
may have such a skeptical opinion that you don't even give yourself
credit for any acceptable achievement. Do you have tolerance for
others but unattainable standards for yourself?

Colette Dowling, author of a best-selling book that was trans-
lated into seventeen languages, said of herself: "I'd always imagined
that a big enough success would settle things once and for all, that
my shaky self-regard would stabilize, and I'd never feel anxious
again." Instead, she said, after the success of her book she was puzzled
by her still frail sense of self-esteem. She thought, "How much must I
achieve to be good enough for myself?" and "Where do women get
this need to be perfect?"[1]

Each good thing we accomplish needs to be appreciated, even ap-
plauded, by ourselves first. Without going overboard and becoming
proud, we need to be tolerant, honest, and loving about our own
worth. Feelings of self-approval are essential to our happiness and to
healthy relationships. To increase regard for ourselves we need to

begin with low-key, believable praise of our good qualities. Perhaps we can honestly say:

"I am trying."

"I work hard."

"Life has not been easy, but I've put a lot of effort into it."

"I care about others."

"There have been some hard knocks in my life, but I have dealt with many of them and survived."

Begin to make your self-talk positive so that it will raise your self-esteem. Remember, it takes time to change, so be persistent and you will finally master giving yourself good ratings.

Your Natural-Born Worth

So often our self-image is tied to countless cosmetic items rather than to our inherent value. You may have formed your self-concept through one or more of the following:

—The opinions of other people
—How good a housekeeper you are
—How much you weigh
—How well you did in school
—How attractive you look

A black minister who had helped many people and who had a good opinion of himself was asked how he had maintained this positive position as a child—a child who had often encountered the demeaning experiences of racism. He explained that his grandmother, who was born a slave, told him the same story over and over. As a child she had gone to religious services on the plantation where she lived. Monthly a slave preacher came to instruct them. He always concluded his sermon with words similar to these: "I know you have many heartrending problems, but remember, you are not a slave, you are not a black, you are a child of God." The grandmother helped her grandson to internalize that feeling just as she had done herself, and it gave him great strength. The world around him was never able to destroy his feeling of self-worth.

Ideally we should all assess ourselves from a point of view similar to this man's. Instead we sometimes put our self-image in the control of others. We try to please others to such an extent that their judgment is more important in our eyes than our own opinion.

In some cases a woman feels that if her house is not orderly and clean she is a failure, a total loss. She forgets her hard work and the thoughtful, caring service she gives and instead ties her esteem to a shiny floor or a dust-free curio cabinet. Even if her home is reasonably well cared for most of the time, on the days the cyclone has hit, her esteem drops into a pit. Of course her children and husband simply cannot grasp any connection between her self-esteem and the condition of her family room. Consequently they fail to understand the tenseness and frustration Mother feels when she can't control the clutter and jumble that follow Valentine-cookie bakes and slumber parties, or the litter of a Sunday without the usual daily picking up.

For other women self-worth is equated with how much they weigh on any particular day. (The only place this doesn't happen is in cultures where big is beautiful.) It has been aptly observed: "The scales don't tell you what you're worth. They only tell you what you weigh."[2] Sometimes a woman can be so obsessed with her need to be thin that she puts off living while waiting to get to her ideal poundage. She can't be happy; she can't go to a class reunion; she can't give a talk; even though she feels she must, she doesn't want to visit her child's schoolroom until she has lost some of her much-loathed weight!

Some women worry because their looks are not in the mainstream. But looks do not have to be disabling. I once read about a man who was known as one of the "little people" (a term for those affected by dwarfism) but who did not let this color his self-approval. He would never talk about what he couldn't do, nor did he think negatively about how he looked. Though his feelings have been hurt over and over again, he keeps his sense of humor and warmth toward others. He has done this throughout his life by turning negative situations into positive ones. Instead of being a player on the team, he became a water boy and eventually a coach. He couldn't go on hikes with the Boy Scouts, so he taught in Primary. Though his wife is more than a head taller, together they have made their life a happy one.

There are others who have turned challenges into triumphs. The famous actress Helen Hayes found her confidence by focusing on her talents rather than her liabilities. She said that due to her military-straight posture she became the tallest five-foot woman in the world.

A Vietnam prisoner of war related how he gained not only greater faith in God while he was imprisoned but also more self-esteem. He challenged himself to find something good in the bad situations he encountered. His efforts helped him to have self-confidence. The same attitudes that allowed him to survive the prison camp help him to survive daily life. He says he uses self-talk and knows it helps him.

A woman can elect to be happy or sad. If she resolves to have more compassion for herself and to avoid labeling herself with self-defeating adjectives like *weak, timid, thoughtless, lazy,* she is surely opting to be happier.

A few solutions, then, that will have a favorable bearing on your self-image are:

— Realizing you can change if you need and want to
— Ceasing attempts to please *everyone*
— Unlinking your worth from your weight, housekeeping, looks

Charity

An article in *Psychology Today* reported an analysis of the feelings of more than 1,700 women who regularly volunteered to help others. These women were involved in volunteering in close personal-contact experiences. Following their service they reported "a greater calmness and enhanced self-worth." They found that "doing good is good for you."[3]

There are many natural qualities women have that may bless the lives of people around them. Do you know your feminine nature? Are you aware of how much the world needs tenderness? We have the power to contribute this sterling gift in its many nuances. These sometimes unprized talents are women's hidden strengths. Each of us should seek to discover and develop them.

You may have a gift to read people, to be sensitive to what they are feeling. Can you tell what others are experiencing by their faces, their postures, the set of their shoulders? Perhaps you have the ability to empathize. With practice you can learn to use your gift to support and console the needy. Remember, anyone who is sad, poor, lonely, broken-hearted, or otherwise in need of help is needy.

Women have an aptness for kindness and warmth. I used to watch people shake hands with Sister Camilla Kimball as she sat in her wheelchair. Through only a few words or a brief touch of her hand, Sister Kimball conveyed to people everywhere her kindness and warm, loving feeling for them. She had developed this capacity to its highest level.

Another gift that women have is the ability to console. One Sunday morning I was sitting in a large building where our stake conference session was soon to start. In front of me was a family with seven or eight children. The mother was at one end of the group; the father was near the other end. Farthest away from the mother was the next to youngest child—a boy about three years old. He was climbing on his chair when the seat started to close up, catching and pinching his leg. He started to howl; his father extricated him and tried to comfort him but was not particularly demonstrative as he did. The little boy screamed until he was lifted and passed from one brother or sister to the next. Finally he reached his mother, who held him close, kissed his tears, and cuddled him for several minutes. It was just what he needed. Soon the sun shone again and he was back down at the other end, laughing with his father.

I'm not implying that fathers can't console, but mothers—women in general—are usually much better at it because of their natural inclinations. Joseph Smith described these tendencies: "It is natural for females to have feelings of charity and benevolence."[4] The ability to nurture does not bring applause from the world, but because it tenderly lifts so many lives it is probably one of the most significant talents you have. Seek to cultivate it.

Finally, another rich ability women have is to be spiritually minded. Being spiritually minded means that it is natural for you to take the high road in your decisions and thoughts and actions. It is an inherent purity which you have the power to diminish or enlarge. Again quoting from the Prophet Joseph: "If you live up to your privileges, the angels cannot be restrained from being your associates."[5] When you develop this inclination you become selfless and can find joy in helping those who feel rejected and sorrowful. The world hungers for tenderness and, with it, depth of spiritual love. Heavenly Father has blessed his daughters with these distinct and matchless talents. Ours is the responsibility to find them and use—not hide —them.

In our efforts to nurture others it is important to dwell on our positive experiences, our successful accomplishments, and the encouraging responses of others rather than on mistakes or failures. This is another value of self-talk. Complimenting and appreciating ourselves builds us in our own eyes and causes us to have a positive self-concept. Likewise, negative reactions cause us to doubt our worth.

Our self-concept has a most important bearing on our ability to have rewarding relationships and satisfying friendships. The ability to love ourselves begins with the experience of having been loved and cherished. It develops and increases in the ongoing occurrence of self-appreciation and is aided by positive feedback from approving family, friends, and associates. Once we truly come to love ourselves, we are ready to reach out and establish meaningful relationships with those around us.

7

Between Husband and Wife

If you are married, of all your relationships the tie with your husband is the one to focus on and enrich first. It has been wisely observed that "the most effective and efficient way to enrich families is to focus on the husband-wife relationship."[1] And Brent Barlow adds, "The simple truth for most of us is, 'as goes the marriage so goes the family.' "[2] Efforts to more effectively communicate with your spouse can bring significant improvement to your marriage whether you are seeking to enhance a sound one or heal a fragile one.

When a bride and groom marry, each comes to the union with dissimilar backgrounds. Through living with and observing parents, each has learned to have expectations of what the roles of husband and wife should include. In his book *Couples*, Dr. Carlfred Broderick tells of an experience that took place in the early years of his marriage. He and his wife had known each other since kindergarten. Engaged for a year and a half, they were sure they understood each other's expectations. However, when he became sick for the first time after their marriage, it was apparent they had no understanding of each other's expectations concerning the handling of an illness. His mother had thoroughly conditioned him to go to bed immediately, to expect to be waited on, and to drink copious quantities of juice during such a crucial and harrowing experience. To his dismay his wife seemed rather nonchalant over his mild case of flu. She simply left him alone until he, terribly hurt and "moaning and groaning and being dehydrated before her very eyes," asked if they didn't have any juice.

She cheerfully responded that she would bring him some. But he couldn't believe it when she brought a four-ounce glass instead of a twelve-ounce one like his mother always gave him. To add to his distress, she didn't even hover near with a pitcher to refill the glass. There was no forthcoming communication about the cause of his anguish, and for some time this same procedure characterized each illness. He goes on to describe what finally happened:

> At last, my wife said to me one day with tears in her eyes, "What is it with you and juice? I don't think I can stand to go through another illness with you. It's like a bad dream. You are constantly groaning and grousing about juice. But when I get it for you, it doesn't do any good. What is it you want?" So I tried to explain to her what juice meant to me when I was sick. Actually, I had never put the concept into words before, and the more clearly I explained it the sillier it sounded. It spoiled sickness for me for good. I have rarely missed a day of work since.[3]

It seems that these two had learned different ideas in their "families-of-origin."[4] One had been taught, or at least had observed, that in times of sickness a person retired from the family, and other members left him in privacy to get well. That was how caring was shown. The other had learned that a sick person should be zealously nurtured, that is, given an extra measure of attention. In such a situation, if neither partner recognized the differences in their conditioning, each could be terribly hurt in times of sickness by being treated exactly opposite of what he or she was most comfortable with.

All of this underscores the observation made by Virginia Satir: "Familiarity exerts a powerful pull. Most people will choose the familiar, even though uncomfortable, over the unfamiliar. . . . People often work out marriages similar to their own parents'. "[5]

Differing expectations come not only from family routines but also from educational, cultural, and religious practices. These influences affect many areas of a relationship. It is vital to discuss the tensions they may cause. Sometimes these differences in outlook are not discovered for years; when they are, suddenly many past puzzles and conflicts are explained.

The better a husband and wife communicate, the better they understand each other. Five ways we can build and improve communication in our marriages are:

1. Show appreciation to each other
2. Speak together frequently
3. Speak with courtesy and caring
4. Speak honestly and frankly about feelings
5. Deepen commitment; spend more time together

Appreciation

Showing appreciation is a way to cherish your husband. Your verbal approval and commendation will lift and help him. Thank him for taking out the garbage, for putting gas in the car, or for writing the checks to pay the bills. Seek every day for something on which to sincerely compliment him. Compliment him on being cheerful, playing with the children, and taking you to the movie. Husbands shouldn't have to bring roses before they are appreciated.

On the other hand, your criticism or sarcasm or belittling of your husband can cut and tear him down in a way which is most detrimental. Surely the way to build your husband is not to remind him of his shortcomings but rather to see and prize the things he does well or tries to do well. Your compliments, if genuine and specific, will have a greater effect on his self-esteem, as well as on his accomplishments, than anything he hears from anyone else in this world.

One psychologist, Irene Vogel, suggests that a good practice to restore a couple's esteem for one another is to exchange compliments for five minutes each evening. "It may sound contrived, but couples who haven't said anything nice to each other for a long time are amazed at how many things they still like about each other."[6] When complimenting your husband, remember that sincerity is a must.

Frequent Communication

The next step is to speak together frequently. I knew a young couple who gradually developed difficulties in their relationship. When they had been married about six years they perceived that the problem was becoming very serious, so they began seeing a marriage counselor from LDS Social Services. After they had two or three appointments with him, he told them he thought their main problem was communication.

The first suggestion he gave was for them to set aside thirty minutes a day to talk and visit. For the first fifteen minutes the wife would tell her husband what had happened to her that day; for the second fifteen minutes the husband would describe his experiences of the day. They were to sit near each other, even with their knees touching. They were to continue these visits for a number of weeks —until they learned to talk to each other spontaneously.

Soon after they started this therapy they came to realize that it had been a long time since they had done much talking, except about necessities. They had enjoyed chatting and visiting in the early period of their marriage, but after the babies came and began to require so much of the couple's time and effort, they had gradually lapsed into silence when they were together. Consequently they knew little about one another's feelings, frustrations, or hopes. They had lost their understanding of one another.

Men and women are quite different in some of their needs. If we each try to understand the other we can more truly fill one another's needs and wants. Surveys have established that one difference is that when men feel hurt or lonely and want an affirmation of love from their wives, physical or sexual closeness has the greatest meaning for them. Women, in the same situation, yearn for emotional closeness, for talking, and for understanding of their feelings from their husbands. Each will respond to both ways of showing love, but understanding the partner's *primary* needs gives the spouse a chance to be unselfish and tender in more meaningful ways. A rebuff of a primary need of the other may cause a deep wound. This is an area for thoughtful talks between partners.

Courtesy and Caring

To speak with courtesy and caring is vital. The tone of a conversation is as important as the clarity of its message. Anger and hostility beget harsh responses; but a "soft answer," which we learn about in Proverbs 15:1, is really very soothing and relaxing to a companion. The habit of saying everything with a pleasant inflection can be cultivated. Your words and tone will have great sway over the climate of your home. Of course, though we wish we could always control our voices, there will be times we fail, but with effort we'll be successful more and more of the time.

Some men and women bring great sorrow to their spouses by not controlling themselves when they are angry. They say vindictive words such as "I hate you!" or "I wish we had never married!" Later, when they have regained composure, they expect these words to be forgotten and the relationship to be restored. They may believe that their mates understand that they didn't really mean what they said earlier. But the marriage will be at risk because of such words. It will be hard to regain trust; the wounds will still be there, though covered over. It is important for us to control ourselves and not utter words of anger and hurt, for they do jeopardize the whole relationship. Once we learn to control our words the next step is to make the effort to rid ourselves of vengeful thoughts.

Another time a woman can show caring for her husband is when they are with others. If she tells stories that embarrass or hurt her husband, how can he feel that he means more to her than the laugh she may get? It isn't right to criticize one's companion to outsiders, nor is it right to complain to others of his shortcomings. If the problems are too large for you and your partner to overcome, seek help from your bishop or a recommended family counselor. If your husband is unwilling to go, go alone. You may learn enough to start a healing, enough to help him want to go. Many good marriages can be saved if help is sought early enough.

Honesty and Frankness

As was illustrated by the comical story, mentioned earlier in this chapter, about the husband who had the flu and expected a lot of attention and juice, a tendency for neither partner to speak to the other about the concerns he or she feels can be a real stickler in a relationship! Perhaps there is fear that talking frankly about feelings will bring strain and hurt to the other. There *is* risk involved, but surely it is not as great as the danger of building walls of misunderstanding. It is better to deal with reappearing problems than to let them develop into crises.

As we address recurring difficulties in our relationships, we will gain tact and eventually develop know-how. In our honesty we need to disclose our own feelings in a way that is sensitive to the other person. We can make positive self-disclosures without being blunt or brutal. Self-disclosure refers to feelings we have but that the other person cannot know of until we explain them. Between mature individuals the dividends of learning to speak honestly but tactfully are precious and can bring them closer to one another.

The way to learn to speak frankly is to talk in terms that will not wound. A good rule is not to label someone and not to attack the person's character. We should realize that if we call someone "clumsy," "messy," "lazy," or a "loser," there is no need to continue speaking to them, because they will no longer be listening.

Suppose you know better than to say, "Oh, you always get your feelings hurt so easily! Are you offended again?" and instead try to make a less threatening statement such as, "You seem moody." You still have lost the attention of the person you are addressing, because you have labeled him. The terms *always* and *never* also should be avoided; they are most likely untrue, and the anger they cause obstructs further discussion.

More productive than labeling or name-calling is describing how the disputed action has made you feel. That is, send "I" messages rather than "you" messages. For example, instead of saying, "You make me angry when you don't get home in time for dinner," you might say, "I feel anxious when I don't hear from you and it is long past dinnertime." Rather than saying, "You make me furious when you leave all your hunting gear in the car and bring it home with the gas tank empty," it would be better to observe, "I feel embarrassed when my friends have to ride in a dirty car," or "I'm worried I will be caught in traffic before I can get any gas." Usually we do not antagonize our companions when we courteously, not accusingly, describe our own feelings.

Couples who have confrontations often turn the knife in the wound by getting into a pattern of bringing up old hurts and quarrels and going over and over them. I remember a wife whose husband made the mistake of forgetting her on the Mother's Day after their first baby was born. Ten years later she was still telling the story to embarrass him. If similar problems exist in your relationship, you may want to discuss them at a time when you are both in a calm mood. Make a truce to leave alone any complaint that is more than a week old.

Another plan worth testing would be to try to see yourself in the way your spouse sees you. The question, "What is it like to be married to me?"[7] might help you do this. You could consider it together, and each of you could silently ask it of yourselves again and again in different situations that arise. For example, if you find yourselves talking heatedly to each other, listen to yourself and ask that question. When you have complaints, listen again and ask, "What is it like to be married to me?" If you make an effort to use it, this question can help you gain a greater understanding of your spouse.

Commitment and Time Together

In every marriage there are tensions and potential conflicts. It is normal to have them. Bruce Hafen explains that "the difference between a successful and an unsuccessful marriage is not in whether there are such times of tension, but in whether and how the tensions are resolved." He goes on to discuss the need for commitment in marriage:

> Many who experience marital differences elect to leave the scene of the conflict by either literally or figuratively divorcing themselves from the person they view as the source of their frustrations. Many of these in time will marry another person, only to find another set of conflicts and frustrations. . . . [They believe] they are entitled to live without the inconvenience and stress of dealing with points of view different from their own. Often their cry will be, "I'm entitled to a little happiness." If so, they do not realize that happiness is found through the maturing of a relationship based on commitment and self-sacrifice, not by running away from the demanding experiences that give meaning to a relationship.[8]

Make a commitment to use patterns of clear communication through showing appreciation for each other and speaking together frequently and with courtesy and caring as well as frankness. This will help you resolve those demanding experiences and lessen stress enough to inspire patience toward each other.

Finally, take special care to plan time for your companion. Don't give only your leftovers to your spouse—most people seldom have leftover time. Get yourself on his calendar, perhaps for an early morning walk or a visit at the end of your day. Also make time to go out weekly—just the two of you—even if you are unable to spend money. Enjoy pleasant activities and conversations together. Making time for each other builds a bond of love and helps you cleave to one another (see D&C 42:22). It gives you the opportunity to create good memories together, to be lighthearted, to laugh and play together, to have honest discussions, and to share your innermost thoughts.

8

Communicating with Children

From my own experience I have learned that a study of communication can contribute much to parent-child relationships. The effort to learn better methods of communicating with children—showing them respect, asking for their opinions, listening to them, having one-on-one talks, managing discipline, coping with anger, and overcoming the use of criticism—may bring added understanding and harmony into a home and make a whole family happier.

When a young couple become parents for the first time and the newborn baby is put into their arms, wonderful dreams go through their minds. But, practically speaking, if they were to visualize the puzzles and complications which will arise as this little one grows and becomes an independent person they would feel at risk. But the baby is so helpless that it's hard for the parents to imagine that they could ever have problems in their relationship with their child, either in building rapport or communicating.

As children mature however, these difficulties become apparent. Do you feel there may be better ways than you presently know of to interact with your children? Some new, tactful approaches unknown to earlier generations have been developed in the last two decades. You may decide that you would benefit from using some of these pathways of communication and that your need for improvement is great enough to warrant learning new ways. New ways may be learned if you want to change and make an effort to do so. You do not have to be like the scorpion in the following little fable told by William G. Dyer:

> [A] scorpion [once] asked a frog to carry him across a stream. "No," said the frog, "you'll sting me if I do." "Of course not," replied the scorpion, "for if I do, you will sink and we will both be lost." At that the frog agreed and began to ferry the scorpion across the water. In the middle of the stream the scorpion suddenly jabbed the frog with a fatal sting. With his last breath the frog asked, "Why did you do it?" Replied the scorpion, "It's in my nature."[1]

The scorpion implied he couldn't change his nature, but *we* can change—even habits we've had for years. There are some techniques which can be learned and others which need to be unlearned. If the mother and father of that new baby would learn the safe pathways and unlearn the stumbling blocks to a loving relationship, a great deal of heartache could be eliminated. We will discuss the stumbling blocks first, the pathways second.

Stumbling Blocks in Parent-Child Communication

Stumbling blocks can occur when we discipline, when we are angry with, and when we criticize our children.

Discipline

Communication is not entirely verbal; some of the most vital ideas and examples we communicate occur nonverbally. Thus it is that many discipline patterns are not totally administered through speaking.

Many barriers, or stumbling blocks, between parent and child are encountered in the process of correction or discipline. Sometimes we show power through ordering, commanding, or threatening. Other times we shame or label our children. These methods of attack build a wall between us. Therefore, to achieve our objective—to teach children certain limits which are for their safety and also to assist them in developing self-control—and at the same time keep our children's love and respect, we need to master disciplinary techniques which are void of domination or violence.

In our family we have an almost eight-year break between the fourth and fifth child. With our first four children part of our discipline included spanking; with our fifth, it was virtually eliminated. The children seemed to turn out equally obedient. I don't really think our youngest child was less challenging than our older ones; we were just older and more mature. Let me tell you how it happened.

When we were expecting a baby after so many years our friends would often ask, "How are you going to childproof your home? You're going to have to make a lot of changes." They were speaking particularly of the breakable objects in the living room. After the baby came it seemed that in no time she was walking, though I really should say running. She didn't slow to a walk until much later, as she was very lively.

One evening, when she was about a year old, I went into the living room to check on her and came upon an interesting sight. My husband was sitting in an easy chair; she was running around the room stopping at each ceramic, lamp, or piece of furniture. Each time she stopped she would look at her dad: if the object she had stopped at was fragile he would look solemn and shake his head; if it was a chair she could climb on he would smile and nod and she would laugh and run on to the next. He said, "Keri understands exactly what I mean—that some things can be touched and others are off-limits." It was a game he played with her until he communicated to her the rules—and he did so without a single spanking. We never put any of the delicate decorations away, and not one was broken.

After studying the huge amount of family violence in our country, and that which has occurred in some LDS families also, one professor of social work and her husband decided that there would be no more spankings in their home. Much research suggests that violence or spanking in the family begets violence in the child. Think of the logic involved—when a child hits another child and then is spanked for it by a parent, the message would seem to be, as Murray Straus points out, that "it's very wrong to hit people, but when something's really wrong, you hit people to correct it."[2]

Another voice raised in favor of *not* using spanking as a means of punishment is the National Committee for Prevention of Child Abuse. Their pamphlet *How to Teach Your Children Discipline* suggests many forms of correction but strongly discourages spanking.

Some young people who are now incorrigible and violent received very severe punishments as small children. Children learn from their parents' example. Discipline can almost always be taught by peaceful communication methods. Sometimes the big guns of physical punishment are used when a simple explanation of what is best would correct the problem.

At the airport I once saw a father discipline two children, a boy about four and a girl about three. The man and his wife had obviously come with the children to meet the grandparents. They all were waiting for the luggage at the carousel, which was not yet moving. Of course the children were fascinated; they began to climb onto it. The father ordered them off. When they did not move fast enough to please him, he spanked them and made them stand with their backs to the now-moving carousel until the luggage was retrieved. If he had exhibited patience, explaining to the children the danger and then holding their hands for a time while they stood and watched together, they would have soon become accustomed to the situation, and all involved would have felt happier.

Parents must be especially patient when disciplining toddlers. One type of discipline suggested for toddlers is to give them safe, acceptable choices when possible. Another means is to distract them when they wish to do dangerous things. If they do inappropriate things, such as going out into the street, you should explain why the action is undesirable and then take them away. This sequence should be repeated each time the action occurs, until appropriate behavior is learned. (For us, our fifth daughter's going out into the street as a toddler was the only situation with her in which we resorted to a spank on the legs.)

Preschoolers should be allowed to explore, to keep their native curiosity, but at the same time they should be carefully taught certain limits and closely protected. When you communicate with your children, results are improved if you kneel down so as to be at eye level with them.

School-age children should be allowed to help set their own limits and controls and to help affix fair punishments consisting of loss of privileges. Another method that they, and also younger children, will respond to is a time-out period spent alone in a room. The time set depends on the age of the child, but it is unnecessary to impose very long periods. A young child requires only three to five minutes to change moods. Too long a time-out defeats the purpose. Kindness, firmness, reason, and clear communication must be used with this and all other methods of discipline.

Anger

Do you think it's all right for parents to be angry? I believe that it is inevitable. Children and teens are irritating and annoying at times. No caring parent wants to damage a child's self-image, cause lasting resentment, or create hate or other negative feelings through displays of anger. Nevertheless some parents provoke their children day after day. "And, ye fathers, provoke not your children to wrath" (Ephesians 6:4). It seems that throughout history many fathers (and undoubtedly mothers) have lacked the communication skills that might have helped their children be happier.

For the welfare of the child it is vital that parents learn how to handle anger. There is one rule that is paramount: *Don't insult a child's personality or character.*[3] No matter how angry you become, you must remember not to ridicule your children. If you observe this limitation you can safely express your feelings and describe how a situation affects you.

Criticism

Parental criticism is one of the most harmful barriers of communication. It undermines the child's confidence, damages his self-image, and at times causes almost uncontrollable frustration and helpless anger. Elder H. Burke Peterson has observed, "It is heartbreaking how criticism can wound children and diminish their self-esteem."[4] In a July 1989 *Ensign* article entitled "Unrighteous Dominion," Elder Peterson relates an incident that describes the damage that can result from such criticism:

Family home evenings were discontinued in one family because members of the family became discouraged by the contention and anger that infected each meeting. The father, who may have been conscientious about his responsibility to help his family improve, unwisely used most of the time to find fault with family members and to draw their attention to things he felt they were doing wrong. There was little recognition for achievement or accomplishments. Even though he made some effort to praise the children, it was not enough to offset his negative criticism.[5]

Perhaps making family nights more casual (letting the children lie on the floor or have one guest over occasionally) and having shorter lessons would make these family gatherings more fun for all. Correction can be given in a more tolerant manner and at other times so that family night will be a productive, enjoyable experience.

Glen Latham, an education professor from Utah State University, spoke of criticism and anger at a conference on self-esteem: "The No. 1 lesson adults need to learn is to be extremely careful with words. The most powerful instrument of destruction is the human mouth." We should always decide whether what we are going to say will be in the best interest of the child's self-esteem. Professor Latham went on to say that "for every ounce of frustration we get off our chest, we put a pound of trouble on the shoulders of the children."[6]

We have examined some of the pitfalls and stumbling blocks the parents of that newborn baby could slide into. They should learn to avoid the violence of spanking, to correct without ordering, and to teach without insulting or demeaning the child's character.

Pathways for Communicating with Children

In our communication with our children there are some pathways which will help us to have a more understanding relationship with each boy or girl. These pathways include having respect for our children, asking them for their opinions, reflectively listening to them, and having one-on-one talks with them.

Respect

Parents demonstrate genuine caring when they show respect for children. Many years ago I came across an idea that has been most helpful. It is that if young children and teens are treated with the same courtesy and respect ordinarily given to eighteen-year-olds, they will answer with responsible behavior. They should not be expected to act as if they were eighteen, only *treated* as if they were that age.

Sometimes when I'm in the grocery store a child will unintentionally get in the way of my cart. It seems that rather often the mother, instead of politely asking the little one to move aside for me, grabs his arm and jerks him out of the way; then she smiles at me. In an effort to be thoughtful and courteous to me, she is rude to the child. But really I would not mind waiting until the situation could be explained and the child given time to move out of the way at his own pace. Indeed, if he were eighteen that is how the mother would handle the situation.

Recently I sat next to a six-year-old granddaughter at a lengthy piano recital in which three of her siblings were playing. I gave her a ballpoint pen, and she used it to mark off each performance on her program. Concerned that she would get pen marks on her dress, I whispered, "Do you know what *retract* means?" When she shook her head I told her that was the word we used when we moved the point inside the pen. "Would you retract that pen each time after you use it so you won't get ink on your pretty dress?" I asked. She agreed, but she forgot a time or two, and I would remind her in a whisper, "Remember, retract it." She was quite enthralled with the new word and hurried to retract the pen each time I reminded her. When I spoke to her as if she were eighteen, she responded happily.

When we remember the simple practice of treating children with good manners it shows we truly care. If you are spoken to in a rude, yelling voice it makes you feel fractious and resentful. You want to do the opposite of what is requested. This is exactly how children feel. Children learn their best lessons by example. Writer Robert M. Bramson observes: "If you want your kids to be polite, you have to be polite to them. You wouldn't say 'shut up' to a peer"[7] — and Antonia van der Meer adds, "Nor should you to your child."[8]

Asking Opinions

Children should be allowed input when decisions are to be made. Just as a wise manager asks for the opinions and suggestions of a valued employee, we should let our children have a voice in determining fair rules; their helping to make the rules will give children a feeling of self-worth and a desire to abide by those rules. Children have very creative ideas, and I think it is one of the delights of parenthood to ask for and listen with respect to their concepts. In this way the responsibility of making decisions is shared, though probably not equally, and those decisions are carried out with an understanding of feelings.[9]

Respect for children's opinions is shown by tone of voice as well as words. Parents can build a climate of acceptance that will allow the child to be open; he can then describe his own concerns and hurts in a way that does not overstep the bounds and lead to sassiness. Reflective listening can help us set such a climate.

Reflective Listening

Sometimes our attempts to listen to our children are inadequate. We may have trouble identifying the feelings they are having, since words do not always clearly communicate feelings. Also, sometimes we tell our children what they ought to do before we have listened long enough to understand what is bothering them. You might say this is like a doctor giving a patient medication for a heart attack without finding out first that the real problem is a dog bite.

Through a technique called reflective listening you can learn to listen more effectively to your children. Reflective listening invites a child to talk more openly to you as you listen in a manner that is loving and patient; you then summarize in your own words what the child has told you. When you clarify the child's message it helps him to see that you understand, that you accept him, and that you respect his right to have his own feelings.

Following are some samples that illustrate both ineffective listening and reflective listening. Notice that not only words but also feelings are heard and reflected back.

Child
"I don't want to go to school today. Jimmy is too mean."

Response no. 1 (insensitive): "Everybody has to go to school. It's the law."

Response no. 2 (reflective): "You're afraid Jimmy might hurt you?" (You have invited the child to tell you the problem.)

Child	Response no. 1 (uncaring):
"I'm really mad that Carol and Nancy didn't come over to play. Now I'm bored."	"Well, that's how life is; we don't always get what we want."
	Response no. 2 (reflective): "You feel left out, and it makes you sad."

When a child hears you explain his feelings he knows that you are listening and that you care, and he will likely go on and tell you more about what he is thinking. It takes practice to learn to converse in this way, but even when you first try it the climate will change very quickly and both you and the child will feel more patient and calm. In other words, you don't have to do it perfectly to have results. If you're sincere you will soon become comfortable with reflective listening, and you will have more productive exchanges with your children.

One-on-One Talks

When one of our daughters was about eleven years old she seemed depressed and uncooperative. She would say, "You don't love me." We felt frustrated and let down because we thought we had been unwearying in displaying our love to her. One day my husband and I were discussing the situation. I said, "What shall we do?" My husband answered, "Well, perhaps we could use something I learned from dealing with the Aaronic Priesthood boys. If one of them felt this way I wouldn't blame him for not feeling my love. If someone doesn't know that you care for him, you have to assume it's your fault, that you haven't done enough, and you must keep working until he has no doubt that you love him."

I accepted that, though I didn't think our daughter's complaint was justified, considering all we had tried to do for her. But I came to know that it doesn't matter what the parent thinks in this type of situation. If the child doesn't feel loved, you have to double your efforts. So we did. We spent more time with her and tried to be understanding of her feelings. Without going into detail concerning all the ways we attempted to help her, let me explain one thing that was most fruitful.

Soon after our decision to increase our efforts I began a new practice. Almost every evening after our daughter got into bed I went into her room and sat in a little rocking chair near her bed. The light in the room was off, and just a dim light from the hallway filtered into the room. We would visit.

Success didn't come at once; in fact the first evenings were very awkward. She didn't want to visit. But when she learned that at that time I wouldn't scold or preach or give advice, she relaxed her defenses. I would ask about her friends, her school, and her activities. I tried to make those quiet minutes a time for mostly listening on my part. Sometimes I forgot my plan and acted shocked or gave advice; then she would say, "I'm going to sleep now, Mother," and I knew I had lost my chance for that night. It would be a while before she would again trust me to just listen impartially.

We came to love these talks. The other girls kept clamoring for me to sit by their beds also, which I did as best I could. One friend suggested that I sit on the floor while I talked. She said that if I sat at a level lower than my daughter, I would not seem threatening or intimidating. I tried this sometimes; it was a good plan. (My sister-in-law, a teacher, has adopted this idea in dealing with her first graders. In the reading circle, she notices that when she sits on a child-size chair the children are more at ease. Even on field days in the school yard she sits on a small chair, and the children come up to her much more readily than they did before she began this practice.)

Gradually our daughter's attitude changed. In fact it took a period of years, but eventually she seemed to be a different girl, one who was helpful and willing to learn. A most interesting sequel to this story happened years later, when she was about twenty. Because I had thought it might help other parents, I had given this account in some of the talks I gave at stake conferences; she had heard me do this, but we had never discussed it. Once it occurred to me that, though I never used her name in telling the experience, it might be embarrassing to her. So I asked her if my telling this story bothered her. Looking quite surprised she asked, "Mother, was it I?" Then I realized we had had more success than we knew; she didn't even remember the time when she had felt unloved.

Besides one-on-one talks at home, find ways to increase one-on-one experiences with each child. You may take one child on an errand. If it is practical you can prearrange to stop by his daddy's work and let him see what his father does. When you take a daughter on a shopping errand take time to eat a sandwich together and visit with her. It is important to have some time alone with each child. You don't have to spend money or take a long time. Perhaps you can take one child with you when you pick up dry cleaning and another when you go to wash the car.

I know a young mother who says that if she takes each child somewhere away from the rest of the family for a short period of time each week, she can feel an increase in the closeness of their relationship. It gives her the opportunity to show love and to increase understanding communication. She has noticed that if she neglects doing this for two weeks in a row, these positive feelings aren't as strong between her and the child.

If your relationship with your child is strained, ask yourself this question: "How often do we have a good time together—no preaching, no teaching, just fun?" Another good question to ask is: "Do we have more good times than bad times?" Often remind yourself to increase the good times. To your relationship the good times are like money in your savings account. They will help you balance out the difficult times and keep your credit with your child high. Beyond that, they help *you* deepen your love for a demanding child.

Managing Stress

We have looked at some of the stumbling blocks we encounter when communicating with our children and some of the pathways which lead to understanding between parents and children. But in spite of our diligence in applying these ideas and our true desire to have tolerance and understanding characterize our communication, there are times that we fail.

Because of stresses and the large number of children in many of our families, mothers of young children sometimes feel overwhelmed. They are pulled in every direction and have little time for self. If this seems to be a description of your situation, remember that it is important to find some kind of release and help. Perhaps you could have some plans to put into motion when you are stretched to the limit of your patience. You could make prearrangements with your husband to take over briefly, if he is free, when you have such a need; or you could make the same arrangements with an older child. You could get some physical exercise—a brief walk or short errand that would remove you from a frustrating situation.

If no family member is available, calling a neighbor girl to baby-sit on short notice may be a possibility to give you a breather in times of strain. Beyond this, try to plan some regular breaks, such as walking with your friends in the evening, so that you can look forward to a time-out as well as keep yourself from reaching the breaking point.

If you feel you would like more instruction on good relationships with children, you might ask your bishop or your stake president about a class developed by LDS Social Services called "Becoming a Better Parent."[10] It is usually taught on a weeknight and consists of ten two-hour sessions. If your stake president requests the class, teachers will be trained and certified through LDS Social Services. The class is available through the Social Service agencies in all major cities in the United States and Canada as well as in many international offices.

You may also be able to take a Church family relationship class, which, under the bishop's direction, can be taught during the Sunday School period. The manual for parents is entitled *A Parent's Guide* and that for instructors is *Teach Them Correct Principles*, both of which are available at Church distribution centers.

The scriptures can give us additional strength and guidance as we seek to establish better relationships with our children. President Benson has told us that our homes will be happier if we are reading the Book of Mormon. One mother of a large family told me she can recognize an appreciable difference in her personal resources and composure when she is doing this.

Just as you do, I believe children should be prized. If we learn to use better communication methods, even when we are tired and weighed down with problems, it will help us have the patience and forbearance to treat them like the treasures they are.

9

Talking
with Teens

In order to succeed in talking to teens we need to increase and sharpen the communicative skills we used when they were younger children. These skills will help us overcome stumbling blocks in communicating with our teens as well as provide good pathways to "teen talk."

By the time we have teenagers we have had some years of experience and practice in parenting; we should be ready for them. I have never felt that teenagers are more difficult for a parent to talk to, discipline, guide, or enjoy than young children are, because parents of teenagers have increased their abilities and are ready to handle complex interactions with adolescents.

For some, the years with young children are simpler. For others, there is a natural camaraderie when the child becomes a more independent person, and there is a better understanding of how to appeal to him. Hence I believe that personal knack and preference largely determine which age group is easier for a parent to deal with. Certainly we can all increase our ability to interact with either group.

For years I have noticed that older parents often try to awe parents of younger children by telling them, "Just wait until they are teens; then you'll know what real problems are!" But I maintain that you can handle each age in its season because you become more adept as the child grows older.

Much of what you learn about communication with young children will still be valid and helpful when they are older. The same stumbling blocks hold us back; the same pathways are bright with promise. But with teens there are different, more subtle nuances for us to adapt to. These challenges are what make teenagers so interesting. In this section we will discuss many of the same rules of good communication that applied to younger children, but with somewhat different approaches.

Stumbling Blocks in Parent-Teen Communication

With teenagers, as with children, there are certain stumbling blocks which force a wedge between parent and youth. These barriers prevent good communication and eventually destroy good relationships. The stumbling blocks we will consider are domination, criticism, anger, and requiring instant obedience.

Our emphasis will be on eliminating these barriers. Repetition of some of the rules learned for young children, given with new examples and direction, will clarify how to interact with the more sophisticated teen. One important point to realize is that communication with our teenagers is very crucial because we do not have many years left to solidify the bond between us.

Domination

When a parent controls and dominates a teen he or she causes the youth to pull inward, to hide true feelings. The parent does not allow the teenager, who has the maturity to discuss and help set rules concerning his limits and discipline, to be involved in decisions that concern him. The youth's ideas should be accepted and used, although at times they may need to be somewhat modified. If he is involved in decision making, your teen will have less reason to feel the resentment that Mary does in the following illustration, given by William G. Dyer:

FATHER (to daughter): No, you cannot take the car to pick up your girl friend and go to your class party. You are still too young to drive at night. You can either walk or I'll drive you over; and, if your teacher can't bring you home, you call and I'll come and get you. Also, since it's a school night, be sure and be home by 10:30.

MARY: Oh, all right, Father. (To herself: Why is he so unreasonable? Here I am almost seventeen and I'm the only one of our crowd who can't take the car at night. And it's embarrassing to have to leave the party—the earliest of anyone. He treats me like a baby.)[1]

When you were young you may remember responding, "Oh, all right," as Mary did. She dares not express her true feelings, perhaps because she fears her father's anger or knows that he will not listen; or she may be hiding her feelings because she's afraid of losing her privileges if she expresses herself in any opposing way.[2] She has little control over the situation.

Some parents begin by controlling the young child and never change that dominating attitude—clear through the teenage years. Though Mary's perceptions will be inappropriate at times, she should be given the opportunity to be open about her feelings.

Fairness and caring can help a teenager have the confidence to express what is troubling him. Parents often clearly express their own true feelings but don't allow children to be open about their negative thoughts.[3] Feelings of anger and bitterness that a youth holds inside can lead to a serious breakdown between parent and teen. Then differences and hurt can sink so deep that there may be little hope of healing. Of course when parents and teenagers make an effort to discuss their true feelings, both should speak with respect.

Criticism

In spite of their knowledge of its devastating consequences, many parents criticize their teens. Often a parent will describe the humiliation he experienced when his own parents subjected him to sarcasm or criticism and express an abhorrence of the practice, only to automatically cut down his or her own child at the next provocation. In the following example given by Haim G. Ginott, a teenage son accidently spills paint on the rug, and his parents respond by belittling his character:

MOTHER: How many times have I told you to be careful with paint? You always make a mess of things!

FATHER (*with disgust*): He can't help it. He's sloppy! He always was and always will be![4]

Attacking, blaming, shaming, labeling, and criticizing build formidable barriers between parent and child.[5] Sometimes it is difficult for parents to be mature in their words. We are human and our children's actions anger us, but if we can gain the control not to criticize them life will be much easier for us all. It is possible to proffer healing balm to a tired, disgruntled, or discouraged teen merely by respectfully listening and responding to him. Following is an example of reflective listening (reflective listening is discussed in the previous chapter) in which the mother tries to understand not only the teenager's words but also the feelings behind those words. She controls her desire to attack or blame.

My husband planned to take our children ice skating. However, Donna, age thirteen, got sick. So only our younger son went along. Donna became extremely upset. When I saw her reaction I wanted to say: "You're the one who always gets taken places while your brother usually stays home. Now, for a change, when he's going you're complaining!" Fortunately, I controlled myself. In the back of my mind I knew that if I could recognize how she felt, instead of judging her, life would be better. I said, "It's very hard to stay home sick while Daddy and Brother go skating, isn't it, Donna?" She agreed. I said, "You wish you were going, too." "Yes," she answered with a long sigh. Her mood changed. She was soon absorbed in a book.[6]

What did this parent lose? She lost the satisfaction of expressing her own first angry feeling. She lost the chance to "teach Donna a lesson." What did she gain? By practicing self-control and avoiding criticism she won the good feelings of her daughter. She created a peaceful climate. If a parent can swallow pride and check the fondness to be right and the need to teach at every turn, the child will probably learn to have a more peaceful personality and avoid some of the pain of resistance.

We, as parents, know that our occasional pettiness can be the catalyst for rebellion. Through learning self-control and humility we can eliminate the tendency to be critical.

Replacing criticism with approval and understanding builds love in teens and teaches them to want to try harder to please the parent. It also brings multiple dividends as the parents' example of self-control helps the child to absorb the traits of tolerance and acceptance of others into his own character.

I remember reading about a childhood experience recalled by a middle-aged woman named Millie. The story shows how a mother demonstrated great self-control and understanding by not criticizing her young daughter:

Millie came from a large family. Her mother's life was one of hard work, and included the mammoth chore of cooking for many people. One day when Millie was a girl of about twelve the family was going to eat outside in the yard. The mother had had a busy day but had prepared a tasty meal, the main dish being a large kettle of stew. Most of the family was gathered outside when the mother asked Millie to bring out the kettle of savory meat and vegetables. As Millie walked out with it she stumbled and spilled the food on the ground. All the children looked at their mother. After a brief moment, during which she took a deep breath, Millie's mother spoke as she might have spoken to a treasured friend. "That's all right, Millie. Those things happen sometimes." She made a lifetime memory in the mind of every child present.

In place of criticizing and blaming we can look for the good in teens and compliment them in specific ways, describing just what we like about their actions. When we give detailed recognition of something a child has accomplished he is encouraged to do better. You know that when you are praised for your work you feel great motivation to perform even better. Our commendations could go something like this: "I felt pleased that you smiled at my friends when I introduced you. You spoke to them easily and naturally." "It was a great help to me to come home from my meeting and find the kitchen so orderly and the dishes all put away neatly."

Anger

One of the times a parent frequently becomes angry with a teen-ager is when the teen does not come home on time. Elder H. Burke Peterson has said: "We all know there is a time to talk and a time to listen. To listen with patience to a young person's reasons for getting home late will bring you undying gratitude. Remember, you can listen to understand, not necessarily to agree."[7]

The following examples show two different outcomes to similar situations.

Author Chris Crowe tells of a time when he was having a con-versation with his friend Brad. Brad had learned earlier that evening of his parents' impending divorce. Chris was trying to give some com-fort to Brad, when he looked at his watch and saw that it was one o'clock in the morning. He was shocked to see how late it was; he was supposed to be home by midnight. He ran the five blocks to his home and found his father waiting for him.

Chris explains that his father, in his anger, would not listen to any excuse and told Chris he was grounded. Feeling that he had been "convicted without a trial," Chris began to argue with his father. His account continues:

> By the time I finally did go to bed, I was too upset to sleep. I was worried about Brad, and I was frustrated that I couldn't talk to my dad about it. I wished things were dif-ferent, that I could have come home and told him about Brad's parents. But instead of talking, we only argued about my curfew for the hundredth time.
>
> I really wanted to be able to communicate with my dad, and sometimes I sensed that he felt the same way, but for some reason, we were never able to connect.[8]

My husband has a wonderful healing comment: "Well, you win some; you lose some!" In no other role in our lives is this more ap-plicable than in parenthood. So when you do lose one—like the father in the above illustration—because you have been critical or angry and said something which wounded your teen or younger child, as soon as you gain control of your emotions, offer an apology. Show some extra love and explain that because you were angry you said some things you shouldn't have. The child will most likely for-give you immediately, and beyond that he will learn one of life's best lessons—that saying "I'm sorry" is right and appropriate.

The second story is about a fourteen-year-old boy named Brett who had had the flu during a particular week. He had been back in school just one day, and his parents wanted him to get some rest so that his bout with the flu wouldn't recur. But Brett was eager to at-tend his first Saturday dance. They compromised. He would go but would come home an hour before the dance was over.

The time for him to be home came and went. Waiting up, his parents began to feel angry that he wasn't keeping his part of the bar-gain. They became very upset and thought of going to get him, but they decided against embarrassing him in front of the other teens. While they waited they listened to music. Gradually they relaxed and were even laughing together.

One hour after the appointed curfew they heard Brett come in. He looked defensive and guilty. To his surprise his parents asked, "Did you have a good time?" They talked with him about the dance for about five minutes; then they said, "You know that what you did was wrong. What do you think your punishment should be?" Brett agreed that he deserved to be punished, and he named a much stiffer penalty than they would have selected. It taught them to give each child a chance to speak before he was judged for being late.

One of our daughters told me recently that she has remembered for twenty years the night she got home late and was relieved to hear, "I know you've got a good reason for being late, because you know how worried we'd be about you." It made her feel good to know that we gave her credit for being responsible.

Requiring Instant Obedience

Often parents' unrealistic expectation that youth obey instantly causes problems. It is vitally important for parents to forbear reaction when adolescents (or younger children) do not respond in the twin-kling of an eye. Parents should be gracious and give the child a brief period to react to the command or request. There are two reasons for this. First, you know how long it takes a grown-up to react; a youth needs a little longer. Second, a teen may feel he needs to "save face." Dr. Haim Ginott gives an example that illustrates this need:

Fourteen-year-old Gideon was playing basketball near his home early one . . . morning. The bouncing of the ball woke up his father. He said: "I wanted to sleep until ten o'clock today. The ball woke me up." "I'm sorry," said Gideon. He bounced the ball twice more and left. Father realized that the additional bouncing was a face-saving device. Gideon demonstrated to himself that he stopped of his own volition, not because of orders.

Dr. Ginott suggests that if the teen did not go away, but continued his undesirable action, the parent could have expressed his feelings in a frank way. "I feel upset by what you're doing!" "I'm growing extremely angry!" These words help calm the parent and also give notice to the teenager that his conduct is fast approaching the danger zone.[9]

One mother gives a third reason for being careful about demanding immediate compliance. She knows that at such a time she is probably a little angry and that anger makes her hasty. When we feel impatient we don't judge the passage of time well. We may judge thirty seconds to be two or three minutes. Therefore, this mother always looks at her watch, without bringing it to the youth's attention or mentioning any time limit, and gives a full two minutes. Usually by that time she has been obeyed.

Pathways to Teen Talk

Now that we have addressed some of the stumbling blocks in communication and discussed how we might correct them, we will look at some good pathways we can learn to use in communicating with teenagers. These are: having one-on-one talks; sharing some of our own concerns and triumphs; continuing to show affection through hugs, kisses, and pats; being calm and consistent; and keeping ourselves aware of the eternal perspective in our interactions.

One-on-One Talks

With some teenage children the time just before bed (if you can stay up that late) is a good time for special talks. But for one of our daughters it was the worst time. As soon as she hit the pillow she needed to go to sleep. So I had to find other times—such as when we were driving alone or when she was having a snack after school—to have one-on-one visits with her. Also the plan to take each child on simple "dates" brought rich, fruitful interaction with this daughter.

Another good time for such communication is given by Dr. Victor Cline. He says that the " 'golden hours' with teenagers are after midnight." All the interruptions have ceased, and both you and your teen are somewhat fatigued. That makes for better talk; hearts are more open and frankness seems more natural. A pizza after midnight may enhance the setting. If you can learn to be uncritical and unshocked and to skip the teaching moment for the time being, unless asked, you may learn a lot and become closer.

There are times when you will have an unexpected success. I recall one such success that occurred as we were talking with a group of teenage grandchildren. One girl, who is typically a sparse communicator, was most interested in the topics and questions brought up for discussion. She became very outgoing and gave several quite mature observations. Her mother sat openmouthed. When an adult in the group tried to encourage comments from the other teenagers, the mother whispered to him, "Leave her alone for a while. This is the most she's said in a whole year."

At times like this, just think, "Serendipity!" Quoting from Dr. Cline again, "Occasionally, I find a non-communicative, morose youngster suddenly wants to talk. It's a rare occasion, and I let all other things go. I cancel an appointment or allow myself to go late to something—because I'm needed *then*. Later may never come."[10]

Sharing Yourself

There is no finer way to give a feeling of self-worth to a young person than for a parent to share some of his own problems, feelings, and ideas. This should be done in a conversational manner and without accusations designed to earn the child's cooperation through a guilt trip. Sharing yourself with your teen is a way of showing him that you recognize he is growing older and is wise enough to give ideas and good counsel.

When you combine sharing your own concerns with seeking a teen's ideas about guidelines for his behavior, the teen will observe, "Mother and Dad must think I have a lot on the ball; they're treating me more and more like an adult." You can ask your teens to help you choose clothes, plan redecorating, cope with difficulties in your friendships, repair cars or appliances, and solve all kinds of everyday problems. They have outstanding recommendations. By sharing ourselves in this way we can earn the gratitude and friendship of a son or daughter.

This pattern of sharing self strengthens the concept that communication is a two-way conversation. By using this concept we can initiate many low-key chats about friends, school, and activities and not be threatening. These little talks can occur while we are working together, driving to sports events, drinking milk shakes, or participating in a variety of other mutually enjoyable outings. Parents and youths need to cultivate the habit of talking to each other often in amiable ways. Sharing yourself with your teenager, as you would with another adult, builds the teen's self-esteem. This practice makes parenthood much more enjoyable also.

Affection

Communication is not all verbal by any means. On one occasion I had the opportunity to observe a family with two sons. The older was about seventeen; the younger, seven. I could see that the father, though a rather formal man, had a playful relationship with the younger boy; he would rub his cheek against the boy's and ruffle his hair. With the older boy he seemed to be barely on speaking terms. Of course it may have just been a bad day, but it reminded me of several mothers who have said that when their boys are in their teens they don't like to kiss and hug their parents anymore.

I'm convinced this does not need to happen with boys or girls. If you will continue showing affection with hugs and not let them talk you out of it, the practice can go right on through adolescence. It just depends on your example. I see my teenage grandsons embrace their parents and grandparents frequently, and when they talk to me on the phone they tell me they love me, just as they did when they were little.

There is an age that kids reach when showing affection to family while other teens are around isn't cool, and we should respect our teens' wishes in this regard. But when they act unwilling to show or be shown affection within the family, just make a joke of it and go right on doing it. Of course, at the same time you have to constantly work on your harmony with them so that they will be comfortable enough to want you to show your affection.

If your teen is in the habit of resisting hugs, you might try quick pats as you pass in the hallway or a touch on the arm when you're complimenting him. Informal verbal expressions of love, given at times such as when you are playing ball or having scrambled eggs, will reestablish some of the camaraderie you had with him when he was little. All these pleasant experiences can be put in the "bank" to draw on when a parent has to exert authority in some serious situation. The youth remembers these pleasant times, and they help to salve over the difficulties that arise when we disagree with the teenager and have to hold firm.

Calmness and Consistency

My grandmother never physically punished her children. She had a presence which commanded respect. Her youngest son said she was "unyieldingly firm." She was very strict about the standards she set for her children, yet she was gracious and allowed them many privileges. When they were growing up in Superior, Arizona, she used to let them have a Saturday night dance in their living room. They had a large rug that had to be rolled up prior to the dance. Under it, for padding, they had straw.

When the dance was over at a certain hour, part of the arrangement was that they would put the living room back in its proper order. Grandmother was on the scene. If they didn't put the straw down evenly, or if they put the rug out crookedly, she would just smile pleasantly; but they knew that they had to keep working at it until it was right. She taught them by her calm manner and her consistency.

Eternal Perspective

Even though you may do all in your power to have a loving relationship with your teen, there may be times when you feel you are not succeeding. Such periods may last for a few years. We have been told to never give up, however, and Elder Howard W. Hunter has taught something that should be comforting to us:

> A successful parent is one who has loved, one who has sacrificed, and one who has cared for, taught, and ministered

to the needs of a child. If you have done all of these and your child is still wayward or troublesome or worldly, it could well be that you are, nevertheless, a successful parent. Perhaps there are children who have come into the world that would challenge any set of parents under any set of circumstances.[11]

A question which helps to sort out the relative significance of problems with teenagers is, "How important is this issue to his or her eternal progression?" Many times protecting your relationship will be more important than forcing the issue. Some of the differences in your two ways of doing things may not be of much consequence in the light of the gospel. Use gospel standards to measure—not the standards of tradition or what others will think. The years speed by and amazingly the time is soon spent and the harvest arrives. May you reap a golden one!

10

"Listen with Your Heart!"

A sixteen-year-old girl described her father as a person who not only does not communicate but also does not listen:

> My father is sensitive to temperature but not to temperament. He is totally unaware of emotions and moods. He does not read between the lines, and cannot sense words unsaid. He can talk at length without ever becoming aware that he has lost his audience. He does not see obvious signs of boredom. He never notices that he has lost an argument. He merely thinks he has failed to make his position clear. He talks but does not communicate. He teaches and pontificates, and runs any conversation into the ground.[1]

Skillful and loving listening can hardly be overemphasized, because this ability is charged with so much promise. When strengthened by unselfishness and patience, it brings reassurance during crises. Effective listening is alive with caring, sensitivity, and respect.

Our listening can become like this if we make an effort to concentrate on and understand what is being said. If we learn and use it effectively, I believe that genuine listening can heal the hurt and wounds in most of our relationships. We can learn to think when we hear and to help when we listen.

Active Listening

Listening is often undervalued because it is viewed only as being passive. That, of course, is a type of listening, but I hope to motivate you to make listening an active hearing-thinking exercise. William V. Pietsch has written: "Real listening means 'tuning in' to what the other person is *feeling* so that we *listen to emotions*, not simply to 'ideas.'"[2]

This means we should listen with empathy. We put ourselves in the place of a child who is afraid, and we realize that everything he says is colored by fear. A teen may be speaking out of embarrassment, one of the strongest emotions an adolescent has. A public worker may be under the stress of suppressed anger. But it isn't easy for us as listeners to be fair and withhold judgment; it requires real effort. To be of the most service, we have to be nonjudgmental. One daughter tells how her mother did this:

> My mother has been an incredible support to me. She never made any judgments about my divorce and has always been around to listen to me or to be a sounding board for the children without taking sides about the divorce. She doesn't tell me what to do with my life but if I'm obviously upset about work or the kids, she will stop whatever she is doing and pay attention to me as if nothing else is going on in her world.[3]

Although there are many kinds of listening, I would like to discuss one type—what Joseph A. DeVito calls listening to help. He explains, "When we listen to someone complain, to someone talk about their problems, to someone attempting to make a decision, and so on, we are often listening with a view to helping them."[4] We may simply be a supportive sounding board to help them sort out their own feelings. We may comfort and reassure them by taking time to be with them and focusing on their concerns. Or we may give counsel if we're invited to. This kind of listening might be called "listening with your heart."[5] We can bless others' lives if we learn to listen in this tender way.

Improving Listening Skills

I would like to suggest four ways to improve your listening skills. First, get ready to listen by putting other thoughts out of your mind. That is, in computer vocabulary, "clear the screen." Listening is a kind of unselfish love; it is focusing on someone else and letting go of your own needs for a time. Try to have eye contact with the other person and try to sit or stand in an attitude of alertness.

Second, don't try to be brilliant or capture the other's attention with your comments. Listening effectively means caring enough to let the other person have the primary position of importance for an interval of time. Instead of preparing a reply in your mind, analyze whether you are completely understanding what the other person is feeling.

Next, listen with a questioning mind. Ask the other person questions to learn information about details you may need to clarify or feelings you may not understand. If your questions attack or are too probing, they will be threatening to the speaker. Use tactful, gentle inquiries like, "How do you feel about that?" and, "What is your understanding of this?"

In the following example a husband comes home and tells his wife he failed to get a pay raise. Two responses are shown. One is the kind of question that belittles; the other invites the husband to communicate more about the incident.

HUSBAND: The boss denied my request for a pay raise.

WIFE (belittling response): When you asked, were you assertive, or did you just mumble? (She attacks his performance.)

WIFE (understanding response): That's too bad! Did he explain why? (She requests information and gives him an opportunity to talk about his concerns.)

Finally, wait! Wait until you have heard all that the speaker has to say. Listen and continue to ask questions until the entire message is understood. Then you will be ready to evaluate. Be objective, but don't offer advice unless asked for it. The act of listening is a way to show interest and regard and may be all that you should do for the time being. There is "a time to keep silence, and a time to speak" (Ecclesiastes 3:7).

Reflective Listening

As mentioned in a previous chapter, one of the most valuable kinds of active listening is sometimes called "reflective listening." Becoming adept at this requires sensitivity and practice. I have found reflective listening to be a very helpful tool when understood and used effectively. But if it is not properly used it may be offensive.

Reflective listening has several purposes: it can lead to increased understanding on the part of the listener; it can relieve the speaker of some anger and frustration; and it can result in the speaker expanding his original statements, thus encouraging true communication.

Some productive approaches to reflective listening are the following:

1. Summarize what the speaker has said as you, the listener, understand it. Don't parrot back the exact words—restate them or ask a question to see if you understand what's been said. You might begin, "Let me see; you mean . . . ?"
2. Describe, in an accepting way, the feelings of the speaker as you perceive them.
3. Ask questions which stimulate the speaker to further expand his message.

Reflective listening will greatly increase effective communication. It is useful with frustrated toddlers, rebellious teens, angry partners, and depressed senior citizens. If skillfully handled it will soothe feelings and promote peace.

Listening in Crises

When people are faced with some of life's most difficult ordeals there is a great need for support through communication, but most people don't know just how to give or accept such aid. There is yearning for compassionate listening. But often those who are close think to themselves, "I don't know what to say!" Sometimes, rather than make the decision of how to comfort a loved one, the person just opts not to deal with it. I remember a friend who lost a little grandson. She said a few of her close friends never contacted her in any way. This caused deep hurt for her at a time when her cup of grief was already full. Probably no mistake you could make would add to the grief of a friend or loved one as much as ignoring him or her. Whether there is a case of divorce, illness, birth of a handicapped child, loss of job, or death, some general guidelines will apply.

First, think what you would want to hear yourself. Don't give advice or counsel unless they are requested. To the person with raw emotions, such comments may seem like criticism. Just be there and listen compassionately. Let the grief-stricken person (and any loss can cause grief) lead the conversation, though you may need to inquire about his or her feelings. Instead of asking only, "How are you feeling?" you may ask, "What are you feeling?"[6] During crises most people will perceive the greatest support through your quiet love, calm concern, and willingness to listen.

One teenage girl told about her uncle who, two days before his death, bitterly complained to her that no one in the family would listen to him when he wanted to talk about his approaching death. They would just cajole him with, "We're sure you will get well and be going home from the hospital soon," while he was grieving and needed to talk to someone about his fears of the great step into the unknown world that lay just ahead. He yearned for consolation from a thinking listener.

In another family three of the nine children had muscular dystrophy. When the first one of the three died there was fear and panic for the other two. One sister remembered how hard the death was for her parents. They felt it was better not to discuss the subject. However, this sister and another one listened to and talked with the two invalids about death and saw, over a period of months, their tenseness subside. One of the worst things we can do at a time of crisis is to cut off communication with a person who is sorrowing.

When you are visiting with someone who is in a crisis situation, try to feel at ease if the conversation lags at times. It isn't necessary to always be talking. Companionable silence is pleasant unless one of the participants is distressed by it. Thoughts and perceptions need to catch up with words, and a time of stillness allows this to happen. If you seem comfortable during the quiet time the other person will feel a sense of serenity and be at peace with it also.

The ailing person does not want to be thinking always about the severity of her difficulties, and so at times you will want to discuss memories which bring laughter and respite. Also, you can suggest some possible shared activities, such as reading together or playing a board game. Offer to bring other mutual friends to visit if conditions permit. In times of human crisis, compassionate, sympathetic communication is more beneficial and vital than ever.

Listening to Extended Family Members

Another important forum for listening is found among those in our extended family. Sometimes, because we don't have confidence we will say the right thing in the right way or we fear we will intrude on private feelings, we fail to talk about what is nearest the hearts of those who are close to us. Consequently our conversations are often shallow; they merely skim the surface.

Ask yourself how long it has been since you last talked with your brothers and sisters about their vital concerns. I once asked an older woman, with whom I was well acquainted, if her brother had remarried. (He had had a divorce and moved to another state.) "I don't know," she answered. "We don't talk about those things."

Of course, some people prefer to keep their feelings confidential. But if you want to learn whether family members have anxieties they would like to discuss with you, you may want to establish the practice of having regular one-on-one visits with them. Another way is to plan a gospel study and discussion session from time to time. Once you are in the habit of talking over deeper matters together, you gain confidence in one another. Then, if there is a desire to discuss other more personal matters, the framework has already been prepared. When you empathize but do not interfere, listening is therapeutic and is a support for those you love.

If you desire more insight on how to listen, family home evening manuals, as well as other Church publications, and the works cited in this book would be useful.

For most people, listening is a major activity. It is the most time-consuming part of all of our communicative actions. We are deeply involved with listening in our homes, schools, work, and personal relationships. If we recognize its value, perhaps we can learn to "listen with our hearts."

11

You and Aging Parents

In Kamala Markandaya's novel *Nectar in a Sieve*, set in rural India, the parents of a family have some desperate needs and decide to go to their son by cart and bullock to ask for his help.

He lives several day's journey away, and though they have not had contact with him since his marriage some years before, they fully expect that he has never moved, just as they have never moved from the village where they have spent their whole lives. With great physical effort, and by expending their meager means, they make the difficult journey. Upon arriving they are dismayed to learn that their son has been gone for two years. He had never contacted them after his marriage, and during the rest of their lives they never hear from him again.

Relationships are different in our society—not just different from those in the culture of India, but vastly unlike those known in the United States only one or two generations ago. One of the greatest changes in American life in the last two decades has been the growing group of elderly people. Among them are our parents. One day we will be part of this group. So we need to understand older people and to be understood when it is our turn to be old.

For most of us, our parents will be a part of our later lives. Our understanding makes them happier and aids them in living fuller lives, especially as we help them serve others. We can be empathetic when they grow more dependent, and we can find comfort for them and for ourselves in prayer.

Because of the telephone, car, and airplane we are probably not isolated from our parents, nor they from us, even if we live some distance apart. We will be much involved with them while we are still busy with our own children and grandchildren.

As our lives speed along, we have the expectation of living for a long time and a desire to make that long life as productive and happy as we can. Many of the oldest generation living today have not planned for such extended life. The added years are too recent a development.

It is anticipated that as America ages she will accommodate her increasing group of elderly by having larger, more easily read signs and slower traffic lights, among other things. We can be sure there will continue to be more older people in everyone's life than there were a couple of decades ago. Consequently we need to gain a greater knowledge of our parents and their needs.

This is not totally unselfish. Remember, our children are watching our relationship with their grandparents. There was once a family who had a grandmother in a nursing home. Each year at Christmastime they made their only visit to her and took her a new blanket. One year as they were proceeding through the traffic near the facility, the young boy asked his father, "Daddy, what color blanket do you want me to bring you when you are old?"

Thoughtfulness for Older Parents

During young adulthood and middle age the roles we fill put us into contact with many groups of people who become our friends and fill social needs. When old age creeps up on a parent, however, many of these relationships no longer exist—he or she may be widowed, have children move away, retire from a job, and take a less active part in church or volunteer work. Many friendly contacts may be lost. Then the family may become the only source of companionship.

One of the best helps a mature child can give an older parent is to become a confidant. Most of the parent's peers may have passed away, and perhaps the spouse is gone as well. Talking over problems and needs in an accepting atmosphere is vital to an older person, especially in times of crises or at the death of a loved one. Even though parents may have lost some mental agility, it is important for the child to give them respect and attention.

Helping Parents Lead Full Lives

Since they still need understanding and closeness, parents should be assisted in forming new friendships—perhaps through religious groups, leisure circles, or study classes. If the older person has learned communication skills she will feel less stress and frustration during this transition because she will have the ability to express her ideas and emotions. Talking with family members may help an older person develop those skills. We know that self-expression is a very healthy method of overcoming stress.

Many times our aging parents need our encouragement and help because they don't feel the same strength and competence they did while they were younger. We can help them adjust to new patterns, just as they helped us get a good start in school, piano lessons, Scouts, college, and marriage. It is beneficial to help them begin any fresh or different activities before they have lost too much of their confidence; for if they are involved in new activities our parents will lead fuller and happier lives.

Younger people should make efforts to draw the older ones out during group events. Have you ever sat with grandparents at a Thanksgiving table and realized at the end of the meal that they have said nothing besides "Please pass the butter"? They are involved no longer in the detailed activities of younger life, and this leaves them as spectators to the conversation. Also, the conversation may be so fast paced that they are hesitant to jump in, unless you make a point to invite them to enter the dialogue.

Older people will feel more useful if they interact with their grandchildren. By listening to the grandchildren they may serve as a sounding board, and youth like to hear stories from grandparents' lives. Discussion of gospel stories and scriptures may be appealing to the youngsters, provided Grandmother and Grandfather have built the relationships over the years so that grandchildren have a desire to be with them.

Interests Are Important

Elder Russell M. Nelson has spoken of regarding "one's body as a timeless trust."[1] If an older parent does not have the habit of regular exercise it is vital to assist him in establishing it. Exercise gives us a natural high that lifts the heart as well as strengthens it. When Mother spent several years in a wheelchair my father would help her with arm movements, leg raises, bending from the waist, and stretching in order to keep her as supple as possible. She felt delight when she could do these wheelchair workouts.

My mother had poor health from age sixty-five until she passed away at age eighty. Something which gave her a lot of pleasure and self-esteem was writing. Most of her writing at that time described aspects and events of her own life. She wrote stories of her family's first car, which was only the second car in their town. She told of taking motor trips over the Yuma desert by way of the plank road which lay across it in 1920. Another account detailed her acquaintance with Buffalo Bill.

You might think that some of those subjects could make for extraordinary stories, and they did, but my favorite of all her stories is about Monday morning washing. Though washing on Monday morning was probably a very ordinary occurrence, I never tire of reading her little description of it. Any common happening can be a fascinating subject to your descendants. Following is Mother's little vignette "Drama on Monday." I include it here to show how older people can be busily engaged in worthwhile activities.

Drama on Monday

by Winnafred Cardon

When I was a little girl in Arizona, my parents left me with my grandparents for two weeks or more on many occasions. Usually it was because of my father's health. They often took trips to Agua Caliente (Hot Springs) for the mineral baths because he seemed to improve there. I anticipated these visits with enthusiasm. It was fun going to town on Saturday for the trading. We mingled with the crowds and saw the amazing displays of fruit and flowers. I was a little afraid of the animals, but wouldn't have missed it for anything.

The day I anticipated most was Monday. Now, this was unusual, because Monday in most families was considered a day of drudgery, of aching backs, and tired arms. It was wash day. At Grandmother's it was as exciting as a horse race. Before five in the morning Grandfather had the kitchen stove hot, the boiler was full, and the tubs had been brought in and set up for the weekly laundry. Our breakfast was more hurried than usual. While I did the dishes, Grandmother started the wash. The clothes had been sorted into piles according to soil or fabric.

The first thing in the tub was Grandfather's Sunday shirt, then the table linen, next the bed linen, the coloreds, and lastly the work clothes. Grandmother moved in a little trot. She rubbed the clothes briskly but thoroughly, glancing at the clock frequently. There was an air of excitement and anticipation in the steamy kitchen. Our goal was a worthy one—we wanted to have our wash on the line before the neighbors put theirs out.

As soon as the whites were boiled and rinsed, we began to "hang out." As we carried out the basket it was a satisfaction to look up and down the grassy backyards and see the other lines still naked in the early morning light.

Now that the whites were flapping gaily in the breeze, the second heat began. I stood by the window reporting the activities in the other yards. "The Neals are just taking in their tubs, Grandmother. We'll have to hurry. The Martins are wiping off their lines. Hurry! Grandmother, hurry!" I cheered her along.

Now Grandmother rubbed furiously. The perspiration rolled off her face and arms, mingling with the sudsy water as she transferred garment after garment to the rinse tubs. These were hung carefully on the line, and then we rushed back for the finish. I was allowed to scrub the socks while Grandmother hung out the work clothes. Then she mopped the kitchen floor with the last rinse water. We carried out the tubs and hung them neatly on hooks on the back porch.

Grandmother couldn't wait to get these last-minute tasks completed. She would say to me, "Winnafred, take your book and sit on the front porch. They'll all think we're finished. They know I wouldn't let you sit on the porch with your nose in a book unless we were through."

I would take my book and rock leisurely on the shady porch. In a matter of moments Grandmother joined me, her face freshly washed and powdered. Tatting in hand, she too rocked, both of us basking in the satisfaction of our achievement. The neighbors were beginning to hang their "whites," and one had just come out to hang her "coloreds." One, we knew, was just starting, for some of her tubs were still on the hooks. Grandmother clicked her tongue against her teeth in unbelief at such procrastination.

The day had been a success, but the "Oscar" didn't come until one good neighbor called over the fence, "Why, Mrs. Bellamy! You and your granddaughter have your wash all out! I just told my Millie that we'd have to get up at four o'clock to get ahead of you!" Unsuspecting, she may never have known that she had been in a race and lost, nor realized that she was a supporting actress in a real-life drama on Monday.

Besides writing, there are many other worthwhile activities suited to the elderly, even when the aging process imposes limitations. One great-grandmother had lost much of her memory capability. Though she had a companion who stayed with her she would call her family and ask them what she could do. When they suggested, "Have you read the Book of Mormon yet today?" she always replied, "Oh, thanks for reminding me. I'll do it right now!" She got a lot of comfort from the scriptures long after she quit reading other books and papers.

One of the last things to remain in an older person's memory are the hymns. Even those who no longer recognize their families can often remember verses to sing or will enjoy hearing others sing hymns to them.

Parents Can Still Serve

Encourage older people to give service in whatever way is possible for them. I recall reading of an older woman who traveled by bus each week to a hospital to hold the children there. She would hug and love the small patients. When she was asked about it, she replied, "I found myself with some extra time on my hands, and I simply decided to volunteer my lap."[2]

Some faithful older people have such a strength of spirit that they encourage and uplift others even with silent communication—with a smile or handshake. One young woman says that after twenty years she still remembers the first day she attended meetings in her new ward. An older sister turned around and smiled at her. From that day on the younger woman has always admired the older one and felt that she was a friend.

The prayers and compassionate feelings of the elderly for others are a welcome blessing. Sometimes our older parents think they are no longer able to contribute to the lives of others, but we can point out that they benefit people in these ways. They can be a truly effective source of help to someone who is discouraged.

The experience that Mary Ann Wood had when she prayed for her husband may be uncommon, but she is an example of an older person who prayed with faith for something which was expedient. Edward J. Wood was the first president of the Alberta Temple, and he served in this position for over thirty years. At one time his voice was seriously impaired; it appeared that he would become speechless.

In her private prayers his wife, Mary Ann, prayed that he would be cured. She asked the Lord to "make me deaf" and restore her husband's voice so that he could do his best in the temple. At that moment the Lord gave her what she had requested. She became deaf and never heard again, while President Wood recovered and could speak powerfully to the end of his life. This remarkable, faithful sister continued to serve as a worker in the temple for many years.

Temple attendance is another activity that may still be open to the elderly. Temples and temple workers are becoming more aware of the needs of handicapped and older patrons. There are always wheelchairs available. Even if a parent does not commonly use one it may help to conserve strength. Sometimes an individual worker can be assigned to the older person. If memory is a concern, the older parent may still be able to go to the temple, because perfect memory is not essential; the workers will help. The love felt in the temple will bring new brightness to the lives of the elderly.

From Independence to Growing Dependence

The elderly choose to be independent. They prefer to live alone for the most part and to keep their own homes as long as possible. One of the most difficult conditions a family faces arises when it becomes necessary for the elderly to take a more dependent role. This will cause stress and frustration to all concerned. The more choices the older person can be given, the better the feelings that will ensue.

Adult children, for the most part, are the ones who give the major portion of care and attention to their elderly parents. A large percentage of parents live within an hour's travel time of at least one of their children and see this child frequently—daily or weekly. As parents grow older more care giving is needed. When this time comes the extended family should be informed so that brothers and sisters, grandchildren, and nieces and nephews can help adult children form a network of support for the older person. Having several people to show interest through visits and listening brings variety and hope to the older parent.

Some parents still need assistance when the time comes that the adult children themselves, because of advancing age or ill health, could use help. I remember a friend who, when she was in her seventies and had had some serious surgery, still visited her ninety-six-year-old mother's home to do some cooking, cleaning, and emotional supporting. She herself walked with a cane and was barely well enough to function. Fortunately most children have the strength as well as the desire to bolster their parents.

The attitude that children have about giving care is crucial to the parent's happiness. I remember Sister Camilla Kimball's daughter and her feelings about the time she gave her mother. She said, "I'm so happy to have the opportunity to serve Mother after all these years. During so much of her life she belonged to the Church more than to the family. Now that I can have her with me and do things for her, I cherish the chance." She often would have a little luncheon for her mother's friends in her mother's own home so that Sister Kimball could visit with a few of them at a time.

Comfort through Prayer

As I mentioned earlier, my mother had a serious disease for some fifteen years. Her last few years were most difficult. At times she seemed to have no physical ability left at all—she was too weak to open her eyes and couldn't see; she couldn't eat and was fed by a tube in her nose; her voice was so soft no one could hear her talk; to walk was impossible for her. It was a time of great suffering. Over and over again the doctors did all they could for her, but no relief came. It made our hearts ache.

One day I thought about a phrase which I knew was in the Book of Mormon and went to look for it. Do you remember that at one time Alma the Elder was the leader of a group of people who were in bondage to the Lamanites? There were tasks put upon them and taskmasters over them; they had heavy burdens to bear. As they cried to the Lord for help and begged him to remember them, he made a promise to them:

> And I will also ease the burdens which are put upon your shoulders, that even you cannot feel them upon your backs, even while you are in bondage; . . . that ye may know of a surety that I, the Lord God, do visit my people in their afflictions.
>
> And now it came to pass that the burdens which were laid upon Alma and his brethren were made light; yea, the Lord did strengthen them that they could bear up their burdens with ease, and they did submit cheerfully and with patience to all the will of the Lord. (Mosiah 24:14-15.)

This scripture gave me a new perspective in my prayers. It seemed the only thing left that I could do for Mother, and I began to pray for her in this way: that her burdens might be lightened; that even though she had such great trials, they might be eased; and that the Lord would strengthen her in bearing them. I remembered to preface each prayer with, "If it be thy will . . ."

A great comfort came to me from these prayers. I felt that the rest of us, her family, could still be learning the lessons we needed to from the situation, but that her suffering was lightened. I gained trust that she would not suffer more than was essential.

When the time came for Alma's people to be delivered from their trials, the Lord spoke to them, as described in the Book of Mormon account: "And it came to pass that so great was their faith and their patience that the voice of the Lord came unto them again, saying: Be of good comfort, for on the morrow I will deliver you out of bondage"

(Mosiah 24:16). I bear testimony that the Lord will deliver us from our burdens if we exercise faith and patience.

For some of us, praying for our aging parents will be the only thing we can do for them. Others of us can lighten our parents' burdens by taking their hands and walking and talking with them as they endure to the end. "To every thing there is a season" (Ecclesiastes 3:1). The season for enduring to the end is not usually an easy season, but if we help our parents by bearing their burdens with them we will make it a good, growing season for ourselves and for them.

12

About Unrighteous Dominion

Some families appear to be ideal. They act circumspectly at all times; both husband and wife serve in teaching and leadership positions in the Church; children are active and fill missions. But within their homes they may have a serious problem hidden from the world. This problem can be described as living with unrighteous dominion.

This is a very delicate subject to address, but I wish to try because of the suffering I am aware of that exists in the lives of a number of women and children. This chapter is written to a limited number of women; they know who they are, and I have great admiration and compassion for them. I want to emphasize that I do not know how widespread the problem is; I do know that it exists in many instances.

Recognizing Unrighteous Dominion

There are some symptoms of this dangerous condition which are clear yet need to be set down because some women have been traumatized to the point that they no longer think clearly on the subject.

The symptoms include fear and a climate of contention and domination in the home. After a woman has had the courage to identify the problem, there are steps she can take to bring peace to her home. A better knowledge of how communication may help as well as seeking assistance from leaders and comfort from the temple are part of the process.

One way unrighteous dominion can be recognized is that it causes real fear on the part of a child or wife. Another is that a constant spirit of tension and blame exists in the home. Still another is a lack of respect and a corresponding lack of love between the partners. If emotional domination is manifest—in harsh criticism, in sarcastic and biting characterizations of companion or children, and in numerous rules which seek to control without allowing input of feelings and respect of free agency—this constitutes unrighteous dominion.

It is the husband's place to preside in the home, but he is counseled to do this "by persuasion, by long-suffering, by gentleness and meekness, and by love unfeigned; by kindness, and pure knowledge, which shall greatly enlarge the soul without hypocrisy, and without guile" (D&C 121:41-42).

It is important to realize that unrighteous dominion can also be manifested in the conduct of women. The same measurements may be used in assessing their behavior. That is, Do their actions bring about fear, severe resentment, pain, or abuse of others' free agency? The positive standards of persuasion, gentleness, kindness, and acting without hypocrisy or guile can be applied to determine if there is grievous fault in a woman's actions.

If in a home there is domination enforced by hitting, knocking down, or kicking, unrighteous dominion exists. You who have never experienced such circumstances may be shocked that such a statement would even need to be made. You may say, "But of course if such a situation should occur, everyone would know it is inexcusable, and I am sure there would soon be an attempt to set it right."

Unfortunately, this is not always so. There are good women— wives and mothers in the Church—who permit this condition because they think they have no right to oppose their husbands who hold the priesthood; or perhaps such a state is allowed to continue because the wife is too fearful to tell anyone about it. The husband has convinced the wife that she would be grossly disloyal if she reported it.

Not only are these women fearful of reporting physical abuse, but they also hide emotional abuse through putting on a happy face and pretending that all is right. Some have no visible scars or bruises, but they have experienced searing lectures full of blame and vindictiveness.

In some cases they have tried to describe to leaders why they are unhappy but have not been understood. One woman writes: "Life can be such a lonely struggle for women in these situations, for if they go to others for help they are most often told to change their own attitudes, to love their companions more, and to be willing to compromise to get along. So she gives up her desires, hopes, and dreams —which would appear to fit easily within the framework of righteous living—to one who reminds her continually of her failings, letting her know she is not living up to his expectations. How can a woman feel she'll ever become what our Heavenly Father expects of her when no matter how hard she tries, she never pleases her husband?"[1]

There is unrighteous dominion in a home if the father acts as the supreme authority to the point that the mother and children dare not voice an opinion or desire. If nothing they do pleases him—if he is expecting mortal perfection—his expectations are not appropriate. If you have no access to independent transportation or money to use at your own discretion, if you are treated as a child or a servant, you are living under circumstances that are not right.

What to Do about Unrighteous Dominion

If you feel that there is unrighteous dominion in your home, there are paths you may take to right the condition. First, using some tactful approaches, make an earnest trial at better communication. Next, look for the good in your husband's character. Finally, seek help from leaders and the temple. If you have already tried all of these steps, consider once more some new ways to attempt them.

Possibilities for Communication

Attempting to truly communicate with your husband may be very difficult, since much hurt may exist between you. But because of all that lies at stake, please try it. There are certain guidelines for communication that may help.

First, there is the setting. You need to prepare it carefully. Discussion of the problem should take place at a time when there has not been a recent contentious encounter. That is, you should both feel as calm as possible. Therefore avoid a discussion when you or your husband is wrought up. Also, you need to select a time that will be free of interruptions. This can probably best be arranged by appointment. "I need to talk to you for twenty or thirty minutes about something I feel is important. Could we do it after the children are in bed or when the older children take the little ones to the movie Friday?"

Most men prefer you to be frank, logical, and unemotional when you explain your frustration, feeling, or need. It is hard to be objective about your own situation, but if you will think out your words ahead of time and even practice them aloud, you may be able to speak in a detached manner, as if you were talking about someone else.

You need to state your problems in "I" language. Usually you are less likely to offend if you tell how *you* feel. When you begin by saying "I feel," or "I believe," or "I need," others usually can't argue about it, because only you know what you feel, believe, or need. If you make declarations that begin with the word *you*, to your husband they may be threatening or seem unfair or inaccurate. You probably won't want to bring out all of your concerns at once. Begin with the one or two that are most serious to you.

Even if your husband has come to your marriage with little understanding of women, by your efforts you may be able to gain his respect. Developing your mind and talents may earn you more consideration from him. Study him and try to recognize his needs and appreciate his strengths. If his motives are good, he is deserving of tolerance. Even though he does not understand your needs, through clear communication you may be able to explain them to him.

By all means, communication is the first and one of the best ways to try to effect a solution to unrighteous dominion. It is valuable from the very beginning and, if learned early, may truly make a difference. However, your plight may be so grave that there is no listening, fairness, or open-mindedness toward your pleas.

Looking for the Good

Another suggestion may be helpful. If you will look each day for something good that your husband does and thank him for it, in time your sincere expressions of appreciation may bear fruit. I'm speaking only of very simple things. You need to be genuine in your expression. It may seem impossible to find an act worthy of thanks, but by diligent searching you may be able to start such a practice.

It may be hard for you to have a desire to do it, but perhaps you can feel more tolerant of your husband if you understand that more than likely, if he is domineering, he suffers from low self-esteem. It is acknowledged that those who commit domestic violence usually have little self-confidence; it is surely true that emotional abusers also lack feelings of self-worth.

Help from Leaders and the Temple

We know that a wife is to follow her husband, but only in righteousness. If your husband exerts unrighteous dominion, and you are unable to communicate to him your distress, you need to talk with your priesthood leaders in a frank and specific way so that you can make sure they understand the depth of the problem. If you are unsuccessful in explaining your plight to your bishop, go to your stake president, but don't give up. You need to act so that you, as well as your husband and your children, may clear the climate of your home from unjust domination. If you are afraid to speak out, go to the temple and pray to receive direction about how you may accomplish your task. When you do this you will be entitled to guidance and inspiration. You may not receive it while you are at the temple, but in time it will be manifest to you, because of your obedience.

Because of your difficult experiences, you yourself may have feelings of low self-esteem. One cause of this may be that you often have to hide your true feelings. Being unable to express anger, frustration, fright—even love or happiness—gives rise to feelings of hypocrisy and dishonesty. The consequence of these feelings is a dislike for self and a sense of loss of integrity, which in turn lead to a deterioration of self-respect. If this is your situation, these are very normal feelings. The chapter on self-image may help you to overcome some of these difficulties.

The final suggestion for help is to go to the temple, as often as possible, to seek comfort and strength. Participate in the initiatory ordinances and listen again to the promises made to you there. If you are not endowed, know that you can participate in baptisms for the dead. These are just as necessary a work in the temple as any other, and adults go regularly to do them. If you will call the temple arrangements can be made for you to do baptisms—it is not necessary to have a specific assignment.

After you arrive at the temple, if at all possible try to spend several hours there. Spending some time in those sacred surroundings will lighten your burden of care. Being in the temple will give you an opportunity to feel the inspiration, light, and comfort the Spirit brings, and whispers of peace and hope will encircle you.

Hope comes as you raise your own level of spirituality. If you are living under the pressure of unrighteous dominion, I only can guess how difficult the situation is for you, but other women have learned much from their adversity, and I know Heavenly Father will bless your efforts.

Please try to use more direct communication with your husband and to express appreciation for his good qualities. Remember to counsel with your leaders in the ways suggested here, and take time to "drink in" the comfort of the temple. I believe these steps may lead you to a happier, more relaxed situation.

From time to time I hear of the sorrows of those who suffer from unrighteous dominion; if you are struggling under such circumstances, please know that my heart aches for you. I wish I could help you, and I pray that the Lord will lighten your burdens and bless you with his peace and the understanding to cope with your problems.

13

Friendships with Other Women

When I meet a woman who is living away from her home and is somewhat isolated from other women—such as the woman whose husband is going to school in a foreign country or serving as a mission president—I sometimes ask her what she misses most. More than once the answer has been, "What I miss most is being with American women"; or, if she is in the United States, "I miss talking with women my own age. I'm happy, working hard, and loving it, but I would welcome some interaction with my peers to feel complete." Of course these women realize they are in situations which are temporary, and they are content to wait, but their feelings demonstrate the need women have for meaningful communication with other women.

Life is so filled with demands from work and family that as women we often let the need for friendships with other women go unfulfilled, thinking we can't spend the time to cultivate such friendships. This happens more often after marriage than when a woman is single. But after marriage, even though our husbands are our best friends, good women friends can support and enrich our lives.

Circles of Friends

Two of my daughters belong to a group of friends who have met together for seventeen years now. They started meeting when they each had very young children. Now some of those toddlers are missionaries. They call it their "Mothers' Meeting." In the earlier years they had discussions about ways to cope with childhood discipline or teach children to work. Now they have become a group of friends who may visit about different concerns—health, budgets, improving marriage; or they may play a game they call "Say One Nice Thing about Sherrie," in which they all voice good things they feel about each other. These women have developed lifelong friendships with each other.

I belong to a group of friends who love to read books and then meet and discuss them. We have met for many years. One winter evening a member of the group said, "Let's never change; even when we are old let's still meet every month and share our thoughts and feelings."

Perspective from Friends

Women friends give us companionship; they give us an opportunity to learn from more than one (our own) family's life and wisdom. With other women we can discuss experiences, maybe even pains, that are unique to women. I once talked at length with a woman who had married during middle age. Her husband, who was an older man, thought that he should be her whole life and that she should be able to find enough friendship and sociability in their life together. She felt a great emptiness and said, "I don't have a mother or a sister to talk to. I don't know if what is happening is normal and I am just overreacting to it, or if I need medical help. I need to compare my life with another woman's so that I can get a perspective on it."

We all need to have exchanges with our peers in order to hone our judgment skills. Everyone you encounter and have such an interchange with teaches you either by positive or negative example. Both are useful; we know we can learn even from negative lessons.

Most husband-wife relationships are not threatened by friendships each may have with others of their own gender. One young woman told me that she and her husband spend recreation time with separate friends as well as with each other. He doesn't like plays or ballet; she goes with her women friends and comes home refreshed and enriched. He loves to spend time at home—gardening or working on his Model A car—and he comes in having had recreation that lifts him. He has a network of friends who have an interest in classic cars.

I knew a woman who was eighty years old when she told me, "My husband never has liked to travel, but he doesn't think I should stay home. I've gone everywhere—usually with a friend, or a group. This year I'm going to Antarctica."

When a woman is first married she may have an idealized picture of marriage; she might never have seen or heard her parents quarrel or even have a disagreement. She expects to live happily ever after. When the first disagreement comes she feels terrible and needs insight on how to evaluate how serious it is. If she has no communication with a close friend or relative she may have "tunnel vision" and think she's the only one that this has ever happened to. When she learns that it is pretty much normal to disagree from time to time, she will sigh with relief and try harder to pass over it.

Communication with wise and caring friends is therapy. When I reached middle age I was unprepared for the great adjustment it took. My husband was as surprised and puzzled over my reaction as I was (when he reached middle age there were not such great changes in his routine). For me it was like starting a new life. I had to find a new direction for my energies—one which fit my desires and made me feel worthwhile and useful. It took me at least three years to adapt to my new situation. When new seasons of your life come, such as having an empty nest or having older parents to care for, the ideas and insights of friends are worth a king's ransom.

Friends bring you out of your own troubles and concerns. A young friend told me that when she was first married and had two young children with whom she stayed at home, she had neither a car of her own nor money for anything extra, and she felt unhappy and deprived. Her father told her of a widow who, though homebound, had made "telephone friends" and derived much happiness from her talks with them. The young mother decided to choose two older ladies and to call them regularly. She said they all benefited. The ladies loved her phone calls, and she felt relieved of her own problems for a time.

Another woman, one who has cancer, has found that her friends are a great comfort to her. Just at the time her disease was diagnosed her husband became a bishop. While he was often tied up in all the weighty problems a bishop faces, her friends helped her to establish a greater sense of normalcy. When her son was leaving on a mission and she wanted to see him off at the plane, her friends spent three hours getting her ready and helping to transport her. It was a blessing to her, but just as great a blessing to those giving the help.

We are the Lord's helpers. One of the finest ways of accomplishing his work is through friendships. All involved are uplifted and happier. We can roll back and forth between helping each other as our needs and trials come and go. A friend once made a ceramic for me and placed on it the words, "A friend is a gift of the heart."

Making Friends

Some women wonder how they can meet friends. Beyond the obvious avenues of church work, volunteer work, and regular employment there is a wide variety of opportunities. One of our daughters and her husband live in a large apartment complex. One summer they decided to get a dog, a tiny toy dachshund. Whenever our daughter walks outside with the dog, many people who never spoke to her before now come up to her and initiate conversations. It is a great door opener. Children also give us something to strike up a conversation about.

When you change the place where you sit in Relief Society or sacrament meeting, someone new will sit by you. Once at an evening homemaking meeting I sat by someone I seldom sit with. I had thought she didn't really care much for me. I was surprised when she gave evidence that she truly does like me. I felt enriched and had a chance to make a new friend.

Another way to seek friends is to look for common interests among those who are a different age—older or younger. We are also enriched when we make friends among those who are of a different marital status, background, economic situation, or religious group. We shouldn't limit friendships only to our counterparts.

Friendships progress through stages. When we first meet someone we form an impression of her. Within a short time we decide whether we wish to pursue the friendship. If we feel that future association will bring friendliness and warmth and that the person has similar interests and values, we may decide to develop the relationship. If we do we feel mental and emotional stimulation and rejuvenation, which overcome the loneliness we may have felt before.

If we desire to progress to the next stage of friendship we must be willing to commit ourselves to spend some time with this person. In our communication there should be a balance of talking and listening. The relationship may be developed to a deeper level, or it may be maintained at a less involved level. Whichever level we choose must be maintained through caring; there needs to be a sense of equal value on the part of each woman—even though there may not be similar age, education, or wealth. It is also important to have tolerance for one another's frailties, because seldom can a friendship survive harsh criticism.

Self-Disclosure

Self-disclosure is a term which denotes a deep level of communication. It includes sharing information about your personal ideas and feelings as well as sharing experiences which will be unknown to the other person unless you disclose them. Such information is usually kept hidden because it has deep personal significance and is private. Before you disclose your more personal thoughts to someone, you must trust her.

When you have established a friendship in which there is considerable involvement, it becomes appropriate to share some of the thoughts and feelings which are closer to your heart. When a person self-discloses she offers a definition of herself; that is, when a woman talks about those areas which are important to her, she lets people see into her character. Not only is it revealing to the friend, but it is perhaps the only way a person can come to really understand herself. As you talk you gain a new perspective on yourself. As you describe your feelings you come to a better understanding of your behavior. It is similar to the new understanding you gain when you keep a journal.

I used to have a pattern of friendship in which there was very little self-disclosure on my part. Each time I visited with a friend I immediately turned the conversation to her and asked questions which led to my learning much about her. But, on the other hand, I shared little about myself. I did not talk about my personal or family activities or my inwardly felt opinions. After a study of communication I decided there was a better way, and I began to push myself to share more. I found that others welcomed this. Now when a friend and I part I can tell we both feel better if there has been a balance between talking and listening. As Joseph A. DeVito points out, research shows "that not only do we disclose to those we like, but that we seem also to come to like those to whom we disclose."[1]

When we share ourselves with a good friend who is, nevertheless, not an intimate friend, our level of disclosure should be more shallow than that which we have with a spouse, an adult child, or a close friend of years' duration. There is danger in disclosing too much; it can lead to feelings of regret later. A question to ask yourself in order to measure how much you want to share is, "Will I feel comfortable tomorrow about what I have revealed today?"

Joy of Friendship

You do not have to be perfect to be a friend. In fact blunders may even start a friendship. I remember a talk given in a stake conference in which the speaker made a rather embarrassing error, then corrected it. When the talk was finished the stake president stood up and graciously reminded us, "Whenever you make a mistake, you make a friend." That was a new thought to me. Since then I have taken notice, and it's true! Whenever a person commits a faux pas my heart goes out to him or her, and I feel closer to that person. I guess this is because making mistakes is so human!

My grandmother was the thirteenth child in her family. In her personal history she talks about her mother. Even though her mother had twelve living children and eked out a living in pioneer Arizona in ways unimaginable to us today, she found time to have a choice friend.

Apparently the friendship of these two pioneer women was precious to them. My great-grandmother and her friend shared books and visited back and forth, wearing a path through the oleanders. They were friends when Great-Grandmother had many of those twelve children at home; they were close in later years when she was a widow with only my grandmother, a teenage girl, at home. When Grandmother became a young woman and rode off to the state normal school on horseback, Great-Grandmother was left at home alone, but she had a dear friend to help ease the loneliness. When my grandmother married, the two friends still had that strong attachment. It was a friendship which cheered my great-grandmother's whole life. "A friend loveth at all times" (Proverbs 17:17).

I think a friend is a rare blessing; a friend (to borrow a phrase from the scriptures) "is more precious than rubies" (Proverbs 3:15). Thomas Hughes said, "Blessed are they who have the gift of making friends, for it is one of God's best gifts."[2]

I have heard a Church leader say that the Church is one of the greatest associations of friends in the world. So, through the many friends it brings to us, the Church gives us a playing field for happiness. In the words of Sydney Smith, "Life is to be fortified by many friendships. To love and be loved is the greatest happiness of existence."[3]

14

Intimacy in Relationships

One wintry Sunday evening soon after we had returned home
from an extended trip, one of our grandchildren, three-year-old
Emily, called us on the telephone and breathlessly said, "Gram,
Ashley and me and Jordan are just *starving* to come to your house."
This reminds me of a couple described in the book *Human Intimacy* by
Dr. Victor L. Brown, Jr. They were feeling great emotional stress,
and after receiving counseling they came to the diagnosis that "everyone in the family, themselves included, was starving for intimacy."[1]
While Emily and her brother and sister were not lacking affection in
their lives, after two weeks of our being away they strongly missed
their intimacy with grandparents.

Some think of the term *intimacy* only in a sexual context, but in
actuality it has broader application, for there is a yearning for emotional closeness in every human heart through all seasons of life. Dr.
Brown writes: "At every stage of our life we seek intimacy as ur-
gently as we seek food and drink. We seek our parents' love. We seek
friendship. We seek emotional unity in marriage along with physical

fulfillment. Out of the love awakened by our children we find ourselves seeking their love even as we give love."[2]

Intimacy exists for most of us in a very few close relationships.
Besides parents there may be other family members—siblings or relatives—with whom one has this close association. Some friendships
can be classed as intimate. For each of us to be truly happy there
must be one person or a few people with whom we have this tenderness and fondness that nurtures our spirit through a caring interde-
pendency. A spouse is our most important intimate, but there can be
others. An intimate is one whom we deeply respect and trust enough
to have in-depth communication with. We enjoy spending time with
this person and also wish to share with him or her important mile-
stones in our life.

I know a family in which the adult children are very close, but
two of the sisters have what could be termed an even closer tie. Their
homes are approximately an hour's distance from each other, yet
they maintain the closest of bonds. From childhood they never
seemed to tire of each other's company. As far as I know, they never
quarrel. Although each is very busy with her own family and church
work, they talk to one another daily. They go shopping and to lunch
frequently together, and when there is an event of fortunate or of
tragic significance in one family, the other family is highly involved
because the sisters' relationship is so devoted. Yet each puts her husband first, and they have their own spheres of interests and work.
Too much togetherness would be smothering.

If you are married, the most obvious recipient of your intimacy
should be your husband. We all seek closeness in our union. There
are ways to deepen the marriage bond aside from sexual love. We will
first look at intimacy in the light of this primary relationship, and
then we will focus on other intimate relationships in our lives.

Intimacy in Marriage

In all intimate bonds, respect is vital. A love that is whole must
include respect—this means that we will never intentionally make
the other member of the dyad feel stupid or guilty. We will increase
our understanding of his needs. We can study him just as intently as
we might a favored school subject. Some marriage partners are only
in first grade when it comes to knowledge of their companion's needs.
Others have earned a doctorate.

A wife should value her relationship with her husband above other priority items in her life. My husband has told me over and over again that I am first in importance to him. No matter what else is on his agenda, I know that I come first in his life, though I try not to take advantage of it. Knowing it gives me security. Whenever he has to go somewhere and I am left alone to do a disagreeable task—be it selling the house and moving the family single-handedly to another state or just doing a lot of holiday dishes—he always tells me that he wishes he could stay and help. I know he means it, and the knowledge warms me the whole time I'm carrying out the task.

In-Depth Communication

To have in-depth communication with your husband you must find time when the two of you can be alone. You need to develop deep communication slowly, because men and women feel differently about discussing deep sentiments. For a woman it is quite essential; for a man it does not seem to be indispensable. When you are able to have such discussions and he discloses his feelings, listen without being judgmental and express appreciation for the exchange of thought.

Asking your husband why he doesn't talk to you, or begging him to tell you more often—when it is not his habit—that he loves you can be quite annoying to him. You can better promote interaction through asking questions that do not threaten—questions such as, "How do you feel about . . . ?" or, "What do you think regarding . . . ?"

When you talk together be straightforward and don't complain or blame. If you have grievances speak of them in the framework of how you yourself feel—that is, use *I* with expressive verbs such as *feel* or *worry*, or use *I* with descriptive words: "I'm upset when . . . ," "I'm concerned about . . . ," "I feel happy whenever . . . ." Both men and women have a longing for intimacy, but many men have only one relationship that could be called intimate while women may have several. You can help your husband to experience tenderness and fulfillment through in-depth sharing.

One good way to start such kinds of conversations is an idea given by a Church leader. He said that early in his marriage he noticed many differences between his wife and himself that led him to believe his wife might be a little strange. Later she confessed she had the same doubts about him. One day he was in a Church bookstore and saw the book entitled *What Husbands Expect of Wives* by Brent Barlow. He thought this book might help his wife, so he bought it and took it home. She promised she'd read it on two conditions. He was delighted. The two conditions she specified were that the book be read aloud and that he be present when it was read. He rather reluctantly agreed.

For several nights they got the children to bed earlier than usual and spent time sharing the book, reading aloud to each other. When they finished that book they got the companion volume, *What Wives Expect of Husbands*, and read it together. They enjoyed the time spent in reading together so much that they got two other similar books and read them aloud too.

They each discovered in their reading and discussions that the strange ways they had noted in the other were pretty common to the half of humanity each respectively belonged to. They found that with a book as a catalyst they could talk about feelings, emotions, and desires without being angry. They learned about being respectful of differences. In this way they began a pattern of communicating which bore precious fruit.

Developing More Tenderness

President Spencer W. Kimball gave a list of qualities couples should focus on to keep love alive in their marriages. These qualities also suggest what it means to cherish someone, and that is what we are really talking about, for intimacy leads to cherishing. He said that the vital ingredients for love in marriage are "consideration, kindness, thoughtfulness, concern, expressions of affection, embraces of appreciation, admiration, pride, companionship, confidence, faith, partnership, equality, and dependence."[3]

One way to develop these qualities is to take one of them and keep it in mind for a year. For example, when you write your resolutions for the new year, plan to give lots of hugs, or "embraces of appreciation," during that year. Plan specific ways to give those hugs to your husband, and discuss your plan with him so that he can help you carry it out. The two of you might decide that on most days you will hug each other at least three times. Planning a certain number helps you measure whether you're following through with your goal or not. The next year you could learn to habitually think of all the qualities you admire and are proud of in your husband. Surely you would never forget these ways of cherishing in the years that follow.

Another expression of affection lies in telling your husband the good things you feel about him. George and Nena O'Neill have observed:

> One of the most neglected areas of communication between partners, and the most important for a loving relationship, is disclosing positive feelings. When partners have been deeply moved by something, or touched by a tender observation that strikes a note of response in them, they should try to express it, to disclose it to the other and capture the moment before it is gone. With positive self-disclosures, that is, telling the good things you feel, husband and wife can open up the way for honesty in more critical areas of feelings and knowledge of each other.[4]

Intimacy in Other Relationships

Intimacy is the cornerstone of a fulfilling, rewarding marriage, and we hunger for it in other relationships as well. Women are usually more involved in intimate relationships than men. Why is this so? William W. Wilmot notes: "Men seem to form friendships based on mutual activity, while women more often form friendships based on sharing feelings."[5]

Self-Disclosure

As mentioned in a previous chapter, we share feelings through self-disclosure, which is another name for the in-depth communication we have been discussing. Self-disclosure always exists in our most meaningful relationships, because it is the only way to really understand each other. In previous chapters we learned that self-disclosure denotes a deep level of communication. It means sharing information about your personal ideas, feelings, and experiences that is unknown to the other person unless you disclose it. In doing this there are some red flags to watch for.

We should use care in self-disclosure because, although it manifests trust in the tie between two people, there are limits to appropriate disclosures. It is unwise to talk about closely held personal beliefs too early in a friendship. We should be prudent in the ideas we share. Remember, they cannot be taken back! If the information we give is of a positive nature it safeguards against our saying things we might later regret.

Taking Risks

Intimacy, as we have seen, does not have to have a sexual connotation. It does always include affectionate caring; it is the seeking out of an intimate friend when something especially good or something traumatic has occurred. An intimate is, according to Rudolph F. Verderber, someone with whom you "choose to spend the most important moments of your life."[6]

In achieving intimacy we will encounter risks. We risk being hurt if the other person is not true after we have trusted her or him with innermost thoughts. Each intimate bond will bring deep joy but also could cause crushing pain. We love our children with a great depth of emotion, yet they can hurt us so exquisitely! Even though we realize this risk, we do not withhold our wholehearted devotion from our family. In living life to the fullest, we dare to take risks, and we commit ourselves to put time and effort into our associations with each other.

Developing Intimacy

Now let us see just how we can cultivate intimacy with a family member or friend. According to Dr. Victor L. Brown, Jr., "the ability to love in whole-hearted intimacy as an adult begins in the experience of having been loved as a child."[7] The less experience we had with unconditional love as a child, the harder we must work to learn how to give it in maturity.

The following behaviors can lead to intimacy because they show our regard for others as valuable people:

—Accepting other people as they are
—Showing understanding of what they say
—Giving support
—Expressing only minimal criticism, if any
—Being appreciative but not gushing
—Listening with tenderness
—Giving messages of approval through a smile, wink, or nod
—Treating other people as unique human beings

The following illustration, written by a daughter, tells of her mother's love and shows ways intimacy may be experienced:

> I remember how I phoned my mother the second day of my flu and was really feeling the lack of the pampering I got when I was sick as a small child. I live 25 minutes away, but in just over half an hour my buzzer rang and there at the door was Mom loaded down with a new humidifier, a tray with flowers, homemade vegetable soup, and some magazines. We ate the soup together, she fluffed my pillows, and made me feel thoroughly loved. Her face, her arms, her whole being spoke of acceptance and warmth.
>
> She was a very touching person. She spoke of her love through little gifts—a new potato peeler because she noticed that mine was rusty—through hugs and smiles, and through the time she took to listen and understand. She always took time to show her love.[8]

If we can learn to exhibit some of the caring which this mother displayed to her daughter, we will have the prospect of treasured intimate associations during our lifetime. George Eliot expressed the reassurance and cheer that come from an intimate friendship: "Oh the comfort, the inexpressible comfort of feeling safe with a person; having neither to weigh thoughts nor measure words, but to pour them all out, just as they are, chaff and grain together, knowing that a faithful hand will take and sift them, keep what is worth keeping, and then with the breath of kindness, blow the rest away."[9]

Successful intimate relationships will bring joy. Those who achieve them are enriched; those who do not are impoverished. In intimate relationships we are nourished. We feel love and gratitude, which bring a rare peace to our hearts.

III

A Woman's Preparation:
Raising Your Level of Spirituality

15

Prepare Your Heart

My husband and I have some friends who over twenty years ago had a baby boy. Like all parents they had great expectations. They had dreamed of how he would play with his brother, go to kindergarten, become a deacon, be an athlete, go on a mission. Soon they learned that David would do none of these things. He was severely retarded and would never move beyond the mental age of three years. They were brokenhearted at first, but they learned to deal with their sorrow. They came to know that David was a blessing in their home.

As David grew older he went to a training school but frequently came home for the weekend. He was home one Saturday when his mother found she had to go unexpectedly to work at the store they own. David's father also had some pressing responsibilities, which could be carried out at home, but he could not take care of David and accomplish them.

David's mother thought of her seven grandchildren, who would be willing to help them, but five of them were on a trip. So she called their five-year-old grandson, the oldest one who was still in town, and asked if he could come over and take care of his uncle, with his grandfather available in the house for emergencies. He said he would be glad to take care of twenty-four-year-old David. Accepting the responsibility, he took care of him in a very mature and loving way for six hours. Surely such opportunities to serve will bless people—both adults and children—and help to soften and prepare their hearts to be Christlike.

The heart is symbolically the repository of our most personal, private, treasured feelings. It symbolizes the center and depth of our soul. Let's consider some of the ways in which we may prepare our hearts to be Christlike. We prepare our hearts when we learn to be faithful and obedient, humble, pure, and loving. We can learn something about how to prepare our hearts by observing the unprepared heart that King Rehoboam possessed.

An Unprepared Heart

Most of us are acquainted with Solomon, the mighty king and builder of the temple, but his son Rehoboam, who ruled after Solomon, may not be so well known to us. However, I think there is a precious lesson to be learned from Rehoboam. There is a verse describing him that has intrigued me from the first time I read it. It is found in 2 Chronicles 12:14, "And he did evil, because he *prepared not his heart* to seek the Lord" (italics added). Additional verses in 2 Chronicles give us other significant insights about Rehoboam. We are told that he taxed his people most grievously and that after he established his kingdom he forsook the law of the Lord. It was in Rehoboam's day that the king of Egypt invaded and took control of Jerusalem. Then, as if in explanation of his life and the iniquity of it, we are given this hauntingly simple reason: "He prepared not his heart to seek the Lord."

How does one prepare the heart? Are we able to prepare our own hearts? From 2 Chronicles 12:14 we get the idea that it was Rehoboam's own responsibility and that it was he who failed to prepare his heart. Must the preparation of our hearts begin in the springtime of our lives, or may we still effect that preparation in later seasons, even in our autumn or winter years?

A Childlike Heart

Think for a moment of the boy Samuel, who has been called the little temple child. His mother gave him to the Lord in his tender years to have his heart prepared to be a prophet. Do you remember how the Lord called his name when he lay on his little cot in the temple? Samuel did not yet recognize that it was the Lord calling him, but he was willing and eager to serve. He answered, "Here am I." When he learned from the old priest, Eli, that it was the Lord calling to him, he was filled with faith and replied, "Speak; for thy servant heareth." (1 Samuel 3:4-10.) We would do well to develop the qualities of Samuel that are mentioned in the lovely hymn "Hushed Was the Evening Hymn." Here are three of that hymn's verses, for emphasis presented in an order slightly different from the original:

> O give me Samuel's ear,
>   The open ear, O Lord, . . .
> Like him to answer at thy call
> And to obey thee first of all.
>
> O give me Samuel's mind,
>   A sweet unmurmuring faith, . . .
> That I may read with childlike eyes,
> Truths that are hidden from the wise!
>
> O give me Samuel's heart,
>   A lowly heart, that waits, . . .
> By day and night, a heart that still
> Moves at the breathing of thy will![1]

Surely a prepared heart would be childlike—soft, obedient, humble, without pride, and loving. It would be willing and eager to hear the will of the Lord. Combine it with a listening ear and "unmurmuring faith," and it would be a valiant heart.

A Faithful and Obedient Heart

Recently I heard a temple worker speak of how she was converted in her youth. She grew up in a home in which her parents no longer took part in the Church. Her home was near the Manti Temple. She spent many solitary hours on her father's farm, and from its fields she could see the temple.

Her grandmother taught her something of what the temple stood for, and she began to long to have the gospel in her life. She said, "The temple was my missionary." She continued, "While I was in high school my faith in the Savior grew, and I had a desire to be baptized, so I asked my parents if I could. When they gave permission, I went to the Manti Temple to be baptized, for that was the practice.

"While I was in the temple my heart was touched by the Spirit of the Lord. I promised myself that I would come back there to marry, and years later I did." She is still faithful and obedient in coming back to the temple, as a worker now, and there she continues to prepare her heart to seek the Lord.

A Humble and Pure Heart

We prepare our hearts when we refuse to take honor to ourselves but instead give it to God. Humility is essential to a prepared heart. Pride must be overcome. In her later years Sister Camilla Kimball came to the temple faithfully every week. In the years I saw her come she never once walked into the temple but came in a wheelchair, beaming and smiling at everyone. She came when she felt well and she came when she didn't; many days she had to bring her portable oxygen with her. She had a spirit of humility which was unique. She was always gracious and unspoiled, though she could have taken honor to herself. She and President Kimball were alike in this quality of true humility.

We prepare our hearts when we purify them. "And blessed are all the pure in heart, for they shall see God" (3 Nephi 12:8). We once visited the beautiful city of Rio de Janeiro in Brazil. In the resort hotels and on the beaches we saw evidence of immorality on every side. In the evening we were invited to view a pageant that the young adults of one stake were presenting. We went to an old, bare building in an area where many Church members were very poor. Most were young people who often were the only members of the Church from their respective families. They had not been taught the pure gospel principles in their childhood but had embraced them in late youth.

That evening they put on a pageant of the Book of Mormon. It was in Portuguese, but because of the familiar scenes and the spirit of the presentation we could understand without translators. Every word was a direct quote from the Book of Mormon. They had prepared costumes and stage settings and had memorized many passages of scripture. How they loved it! I have never seen greater enthusiasm. I thought about what a blessing the experience could be their whole lives through. Though surrounded by the pollution of immorality, they locked into their memories the pure words and thoughts of scripture, which would act as a safeguard for them.

It is not possible to prepare our hearts and yet harbor crude stories or impure desires in our minds. We can purify our hearts, as these youth did, by replacing lower thoughts with the living bread of the Savior's teachings.

A Loving Heart

We prepare our hearts when we love—our neighbor and the Lord. President Thomas S. Monson tells of a particular sacrament meeting he attended at a nursing home. While two young Aaronic Priesthood holders were preparing the sacrament, one of the elderly residents said within their hearing that she was cold. One of the boys responded quickly by giving her his coat to wear. When the meeting was over this young man said to President Monson, "I worried that without my jacket I would not be properly dressed to bless the sacrament." President Monson replied, "Never was one more properly dressed for such an occasion than were you."[2]

I know of an eighty-seven-year-old woman who takes care of her ninety-one-year-old sister in a small apartment. She says she doesn't envy anyone anything except a straight back (she is very stooped). During the last several years she has made decorated stationary by putting tatting on paper. She has sold it through the Mormon Handicraft store and given all of the proceeds to the missionary fund of the Church. She has given over eleven thousand dollars by this means— money, I am sure, that the two elderly sisters could have used themselves but which this woman chose to give because she loves the Lord.

The Prepared Heart

Yes, it is after all a childlike heart—faithful and obedient, humble and innocent in its purity, and full of love—that the Savior requires us to prepare. We will spend our whole lives doing this, and perhaps in the end, after this life, our prepared hearts may become the perfect hearts of worthy kings and priests or queens and priestesses.

During our time of preparation we are promised that our efforts can bring us the peace of the Savior—not peace to surround us but peace to dwell within us. May we be earnestly preparing our hearts, that we may have his peace.

16

Gratitude

Do you remember last Thanksgiving? As you sat around the dinner table did each of you, even the children, tell of something you were thankful for? In your family prayer that day did you especially remember your blessings? Gratitude is often stressed in November but sometimes largely forgotten at other times of the year. It is a gospel principle which is vastly underrated in value. Do you know that being thankful can help you to be humble? It may lead you to be obedient. It can even greatly influence you to develop faith. In fact, gratitude could be the key to your eternal life!

According to Truman G. Madsen there is an oral tradition that the Prophet Joseph Smith "once remarked that if you will thank the Lord with all your heart every night for all the blessings of that day you will eventually find yourself exalted in the kingdom of God."[1] How could this be? Is it true that being grateful for every blessing can lead us to exaltation?

This idea seems to be supported by scripture. In Doctrine and Covenants 78:19 we read: "And he who receiveth *all* things with thankfulness shall be made glorious; and the things of this earth shall be added unto him, even an hundred fold, yea, more" (italics added).

"Glorious" in this verse presumably means to receive the glory of God—eternal life. In Matthew 19:27–29, receiving an "hundred fold" is connected with inheriting "everlasting life."

Gratitude Creates a "Broken" Heart

Why is it so ennobling to feel and express gratitude? A true feeling of gratitude brings a softened or "broken" heart and a contrite spirit. Elder Spencer W. Kimball taught: "How does one get humble? To me, one must constantly be reminded of his dependence. On whom dependent? On the Lord. How remind one's self? By real, constant, worshipful, grateful prayer."[2] Cicero said that gratitude is the mother of all virtues.

Sometimes we may have so many problems and trials that we think we have little to be grateful for. But there is always something for which to give thanks. I saw such an example years ago when we were in the Philippines. On our first visit to this country the mission president's wife had made the observation, "In some places outside of Manila the people have little more than they did in the Stone Age." Years later we found ourselves in a poor section of these islands. I went with another mission president's wife to visit a member family, a widow and her two daughters. They lived in a little shack. They were so very pleased with how commodious it was now that they had enlarged it. Formerly the three of them had lived in one room which was eight by five feet. They now had a room which was twice as long —that is, eight by ten feet. Also, they had built themselves a kitchen that was three by five feet and a bedroom, four by eight feet. The rooms were incredibly small. Of course there was no running water or plumbing in the tiny building. The mother had planted some flowers in a plastic tub near the door. How pleased and thankful they were for their little home!

Gratitude Teaches Tenderness

Even in adversity there are blessings for which to be thankful. When we are wronged we learn fairness. When we feel sorrow we learn thoughtfulness. When we have pain we learn tenderness for others who are suffering. Here is a verse, whose authorship is unknown, that reminds us what pain teaches:

> Pain stayed so long I said to him today,
> "I will not have you with me any more."
> I stamped my foot and said, "Be on your way,"
> And paused there, startled at the look he wore.
> "I, who have been your friend," he said to me,
> "I, who have been your teacher—all you know
> Of understanding love, of sympathy,
> And patience, I have taught you. Shall I go?"
> He spoke the truth, this strange unwelcome guest;
> I watched him leave, and knew that he was wise.
> He left a heart grown tender in my breast.
> He left a far, clear vision in my eyes.
> I dried my tears, and lifted up a song—
> Even for one who'd tortured me so long.[3]

Gratitude Brings Comfort

When your heart is aching, gratitude brings peace and consolation. It has been observed: "Gratitude is the cornerstone of spirituality." Many of you are acquainted with the book *The Hiding Place*. Its author, Corrie ten Boom, a plump little Dutch lady in her middle age, was imprisoned in a concentration camp because she had been compassionate in helping Jewish people escape the Nazis. Her sister Betsie, also imprisoned, was very frail. They managed to stay together as they went from one dreadful condition of imprisonment to another.

They had been able to conceal a tiny copy of the New Testament. One day they were reading 1 Thessalonians 5:16–18: "Rejoice evermore. Pray without ceasing. In every thing give thanks: for this is the will of God in Christ Jesus." Betsie, who was extraordinarily sensitive to the Spirit, decided that surely a prayer of thanksgiving would be appropriate and would lift their spirits. They had just read that they were to give thanks in *all* circumstances. But Corrie wondered what, in all the horror around them, they could be thankful for?

They found quite a few things. They were thankful to be together; they were grateful to have the little book of scripture, which had never been discovered. They could rejoice that the barrack was so crowded, because that meant there were now more women who could learn from their little Bible. Betsie even gave thanks for the fleas, but this was more than Corrie could truly assent to! Sometime later they learned that the reason why the guards never came into their barrack to harass them was that the guards knew it was full of fleas. Being thankful for even the fleas was viable and relevant.[4]

At least in hindsight we are sometimes wise enough to be thankful for our trials and to recognize all that they teach us.

Gratitude Brings Spiritual Growth

Through appreciation and prayers of thanksgiving we grow spiritually. Our Father requires our thanks and our worship of him, not for his own gratification but for the good of each one of us, his children. He knows that through appreciation to him for his blessings we can develop faith in him.

When I was a temple matron, once in a prayer meeting for sister temple workers I mentioned that one of my goals for the year was to learn to feel more grateful through being specific in my own prayers. I had decided to experiment upon God's words, and I invited the sisters, when they knelt at night, to thank the Lord more specifically and in greater depth for all the blessings of that day.

The next week one of the volunteers, a sister with a young family, came into my office excitedly to report her experience. She had decided to give a prayer of thanksgiving each night before she went to bed. Doing this had brought a new, daily awareness of her blessings, because in order to remember to mention them in her prayer she had to keep them in mind throughout the day. Her blessings became more treasured, and she felt happier. Some of the blessings that we take for granted others would give anything to possess. B. Y. Williams penned the following lines about gratitude;

> Take what God gives, O heart of mine,
>   And build your house of happiness.
> Perchance some have been given more;
>   But many have been given less.
> The treasure lying at your feet,
>   Whose value you but faintly guess,

Another builder, looking on,
    Would barter heaven to possess.

Have you found work that you can do?
    Is there a heart that loves you best?
Is there a spot somewhere called home
    Where, spent and worn, your soul may rest?
A friendly tree? A book? A song?
    A dog that loves your hand's caress?
A store of health to meet life's needs?
    Oh, build your house of happiness![5]

Gratitude will help us cultivate so many virtues! It provides a fertile seedbed for a humble heart; it promotes an obedient heart. Best of all, it prepares a heart to develop faith in the Lord Jesus Christ. Will you make an experiment upon his words, remembering his promise? "And he who receiveth *all* things with thankfulness shall be made glorious."

I testify that if you will ponder your blessings daily and mention some specific blessings in your prayers you will be a truly happier person, for gratitude is a holy and sanctifying principle.

17

Criticism Is Futile; Judgment Is Crippling

In the classic novel *Les Misérables* the main character is a French peasant named Jean Valjean. After his release from prison, where he has served nineteen years for the theft of a loaf of bread, he changes his identity. Through a simple invention he becomes a man of some means known by the name of Monsieur Madeleine. As he begins to manufacture his invention he hires a few workers. He is kind to them and even gives them sums of money when they are in need. Some of the gossips of the small city become rather jealous of him because he has risen so rapidly to comfortable circumstances. They often talk about him in whispers and, in trying to account for his actions, surmise his motives.

At first, when he begins to attract the public attention, the good people say: "This is a fellow who wishes to get rich." When they see him giving his wealth to the poor laborers, the same good people say: "This man must be ambitious." After two years the king appoints him mayor, and the people say, "There! What did I tell you?" The next day Monsieur Madeleine declines the office. It seems he does not wish to be mayor.

The following year the king awards him the Legion of Honor. A new rumor circulates through the little city. "Well! It was the Cross of the Legion of Honor that he wanted." But to their astonishment Monsieur Madeleine again refuses the honor. This is almost more than the people can bear. This man is definitely a puzzle to the good people of the small community.

They have gone through every rumor their small minds can think of, from "he has no education; perhaps he cannot even read," to "he does not know how to conduct himself in society." However, the day finally comes when all opposition to him ceases; the people no longer find pleasure in slandering him. He has their complete respect and admiration, but it has taken six years of envy, suspicion, and criticism.

The Folly of Judging Others

Perhaps it is human nature to judge others, even though we usually have very little evidence. But some forms of judgment must be rendered only by the Lord; it is not possible for us to judge fairly, because, as President N. Eldon Tanner said, "we cannot see what is in the heart. We do not know motives, although we impute motives to every action we see. They may be pure while we think they are improper."[1] Being thus limited in our perceptions, we often judge others wrongfully; but if we care enough about them, we can overcome being critical and judging others and instead give them genuine praise.

Criticism is the opposite of love. How can we keep from being critical? We can try to accept the person as he is. It will help if we minimize his weaknesses by becoming his advocate in our own mind —mentally making excuses for him. When someone does something you think is foolish or weak or wrong, try to think of an explanation that exonerates him.

For example, in a downtown store there is a clerk who works in a department where I buy blouses and sportswear from time to time. I always hope that I am lucky enough to come on her day off, because she is very sharp tongued. Invariably she will be critical of me or someone else in the area. I have wondered why she is so often unpleasant. Last time I was there, as she hurried into the stockroom, I noticed that she was limping rather markedly. I thought, "Perhaps that is her trouble; maybe she is always in pain." I decided that if I made that excuse for her I could be more tolerant of her manners. Also I knew I would feel more friendly toward her if I could minimize her weaknesses by noticing her strengths. She does work very accurately and efficiently. Before passing judgment on a person, try to find one more evidence that will be in his or her favor.

We are very prone to judge. Nearly forty years ago our family lived in a certain neighborhood, and there was a couple who lived in the block behind us who didn't have a car. When they went out they would walk to the bus stop, which was about four blocks from their home. Both of them were rather thin, and I didn't think the woman looked very strong. I used to look out my window when I was washing dishes and wonder to myself why the husband let her carry the very large, husky baby. I was more than a little critical of him. Then one day he died of leukemia. I was so ashamed of myself for unfairly judging him that I will always remember this incident.

Judging others is a favorite pastime for some. I am reminded of a couple I knew who lived in a small community. They had no children for the first seven years they were married. It was a great sorrow to them, and they supposed that, without explaining it, everyone must know how much they longed to have children.

They had been going to a specialist in a nearby city for two years to have tests and receive treatments—some embarrassing, some painful, and all expensive. One day the young wife was walking past the home of a family with eight children. One of the girls was playing in the yard and called out to her, probably repeating what she had heard older family members or neighbors say. "Why don't you have any kids? Don't you like them?" For this young woman that question was like turning a sharp knife in an open wound—doubly so, because it came from a home blessed with so many children.

Praise Achieves More Than Put-Downs

Criticism is not only cruel; it is also futile, because it almost never accomplishes anything productive. The following story illustrates how much more is achieved by praise then censure:

A woman complained to a neighbor about receiving poor service at a local pharmacy, intending that her complaint would be repeated to the druggist. The next time the woman went into the store, the druggist greeted her warmly, told her how much he appreciated her business, and filled her prescription immediately. He added that if he could do anything to help her family, she should be sure to call on him, even if it was after store hours.

The woman mentioned the improvement to her neighbor. "It certainly worked, your repeating my dissatisfaction to him."

"Well, no, I didn't do that," replied her friend. "Instead, I told him you were impressed with the way he had built up his business, and that you felt his was one of the best-run drugstores you'd ever dealt with."[2]

Some parents have the habit of endlessly correcting and criticizing their children. It may become so automatic they don't realize how many negatives they are sending out; the child may appear not to listen, but he still feels belittled and put down. Other parents find ways to teach without being critical.

In Doctrine and Covenants 88:124 we are taught: "Cease to find fault one with another." We know how words of appreciation help us want to do our best. As parents we need to heighten our awareness of how much we can accomplish in our relationships with our children if we use honest appreciation rather than criticism.

I would like to ask you to perform an experiment. Try for two days not to condemn anyone. Stop yourself if words of criticism start to come out of your mouth, but count how many times this happens. Catch yourself when you judge someone in your heart. You will soon know whether you have a habit of criticizing. Perhaps you are only critical in your mind and are not expressing your ideas to anyone, but the real test is to see if we can overcome even thinking of others in a critical vein. In Alma 12:14 we are told that our thoughts will condemn us.

Mercy Is Essential

Being critical of or condemning another brings bitterness to us. Indeed, the habit of judging harshly can cripple us, souring us on life and robbing us of happiness. Disapproval and sarcasm can become so ingrained in our attitudes that we are unable to see beauty and goodness. We must rid ourselves of these practices, because forgiveness is of Christ while criticism is of Satan. Jesus said, "Blessed are the merciful, for they shall obtain mercy" (3 Nephi 12:7).

The seventh chapter of Acts contains the account of the stoning of Stephen. When Stephen knew he was dying he called to the Lord to receive his spirit. Then he knelt down, and his last words were a prayer for his enemies: "Lord, lay not this sin to their charge" (v. 60). These words were very similar to the Lord's own words in his dying moments on the cross when he pleaded, "Father, forgive them" (Luke 23:34).

Elder John H. Groberg related a touching story in April 1980 general conference. In the early 1900s in Hawaii a couple and their children joined the Church. They were thrilled with their newfound knowledge and were faithful and looking forward to being sealed in the temple, which was then under construction.

Unexpectedly one of their daughters became ill. Hawaiians had suffered much from diseases brought to their shores by travelers and, as the daughter's disease was unknown, she was taken to a hospital. The following Sunday the family walked to the church, seeking to be comforted and strengthened. In an oft-repeated pattern the father and oldest son were asked to prepare the sacrament.

After it was ready the father started to kneel in order to offer the first sacrament prayer. But the branch president unexpectedly stood up and commanded, "Stop. You can't touch the sacrament. Your daughter has an unknown disease. Leave immediately while someone else fixes new sacrament bread. We can't have you here. Go."

The father felt hot embarrassment, then anger and sorrow, but he silently nodded to his family and they filed out. Just as silently they trudged home with bent heads. Reaching their small house they went in and the father asked them all to sit down. He said, "We will be silent until I am ready to speak."

The minutes slowly passed. The teenage son wondered what form of revenge his father would visit upon the branch president. After twenty-five minutes had passed he saw his father's hands relax; he saw tears creep down his cheeks; then he noticed the tears on his mother's face. Finally his father spoke. Turning to his wife he said, "I love you"; then to each child in turn, "I love you."

He continued: "I love all of you and I want us to be together, forever, as a family. And the only way that can be is for all of us to be good members of The Church of Jesus Christ of Latter-day Saints and be sealed by his holy priesthood in the temple. This is not the branch president's church. It is the Church of Jesus Christ. We will not let any man or any amount of hurt or embarrassment or pride keep us from being together forever. Next Sunday we will go back to church. We will stay by ourselves until our daughter's sickness is known, but we will go back."

In time the daughter recovered, and the family went to the Hawaii Temple. Others in similar situations have, in bitterness, left the Church, giving it up because they were hurt by an individual or group. But today there are many descendants of this great-grandfather who belong to the Church because he chose not to let an offense drive him away.[3]

Pride Is the Cause of Criticism

Almost always those who criticize do it because of pride. They want to put someone down in order to build themselves up. We need to rid ourselves of pride by being wise and humble enough to avoid criticizing others and by being meek enough to avoid feeling bitterness when we ourselves are criticized. Humility can keep us from lashing out and being defensive. If we can make a friend of the one who has found fault with us, we will grow. Edwin Markham said it beautifully:

> He drew a circle that shut me out—
> Heretic, rebel, a thing to flout.
> But love and I had the wit to win;
> We drew a circle that took him in.[4]

President Spencer W. Kimball taught: "The Lord will judge with the same measurements meted out by us. If we are harsh, we should not expect other than harshness. If we are merciful with those who injure us, he will be merciful with us in our errors."[5] There is a verse in the Gospel of Luke that can become our guide: "Judge not, and ye shall not be judged: condemn not, and ye shall not be condemned: forgive, and ye shall be forgiven" (Luke 6:37).

18

In Adversity, Purify and Pray

Each of us has many trials. Some suffering is caused by our own mistakes or sins. Other trials come through no fault of our own. There are many things we do not understand about pain and suffering. But we know we must have adversity, and we know how we should meet it. President Spencer W. Kimball taught that patience in suffering cleanses the soul and that the way to perfection is through obedience. He stated, "To each person is given a pattern—obedience through suffering, and perfection through obedience."[1]

There are two families I know who have recently faced some difficult trials in their lives. There is a scripture that describes what they have tried to do to meet their tests in the right way: "And if ye are purified and cleansed from all sin, ye shall ask whatsoever you will in the name of Jesus and it shall be done" (D&C 50:29).

Blessings Come to Those Who
Seek to Be Purified

The first family has seven children, from ages six to nineteen. The father had always had good employment, and when he lost his job they supposed that he would soon find another position. The time period of his unemployment was to last for a year and a half, but of course they did not know that.

At the end of the first six months they had a family council. It was different from previous councils. Their problem was becoming acute. The parents shared with the children their deep anxiety. They taught the children that if they were to receive an answer to their prayers, for this righteous desire of finding new employment for the father, they must make themselves more worthy. Each individual was to work on purifying him or herself. They decided on these specific things: there were to be no prayers given that did not plead for work; they would hold better-quality home evenings and sometimes bear their testimonies to each other. At this stage the experience began to be a blessing to the family.

At times they felt very blue and depressed. They had to wear the same clothes until they were well worn; every child had to give up lessons and find ways to work to help out financially. When the mother bought something for her Laurels' activities she had to say to the girls, "You need to bring the money for your part; I'm flat broke." But the trial brought her closer to her Laurels, just as it had brought her closer to her family. The situation helped teacher and girls learn to talk in-depth about many kinds of problems.

At last the family's prayers were answered. The father found work. Though it was a difficult, trying ordeal their test was a blessing that brought unity, depth, and sensitivity to the family. Surely it was because of the way they worked at purifying themselves and because of their faith in depending on the Lord that they were blessed with increased love and unity.

"Look unto Me in Every Thought"

The other family had an even more wrenching problem. The father had a disease which had troubled him for twenty years—from the time he was a young, unmarried man. But now it had become critical: the doctor pronounced that it would take his life.

First the family prayed to know if the father was appointed unto death. "And again, it shall come to pass that he that hath faith in me to be healed, and is not appointed unto death, shall be healed" (D&C 42:48). When they felt they received the answer that it was not his time for death, they fasted to know what to do to be worthy of the miracle of the return of his health. They each decided on one personal sin or shortcoming to work on; they also chose one family goal. Their family goal was to have more harmony in their home. Now, those eight children, from ages two to twenty, were normal children, but they decided they would not quarrel or tease. They loved their father enough to make this great effort. They knew they had to be sincere, not decide today and forget it tomorrow.

The hardest part was to heed the Lord's counsel to "look unto me in every thought; doubt not, fear not" (D&C 6:36). After they had worked at their goals for about three months they chose a day for the father to receive a special blessing. In spite of a few slips, they felt they had tried their best to reach their goals and show their worthiness. Two close friends came to give the father the blessing. There was a spirit that filled the room that they had never felt before. They knew he would be healed. They also knew they were not perfect—they would be struggling the rest of their lives—but they knew that they had followed gospel principles and received a mighty blessing. Like Christ, who "learned . . . obedience by the things which he suffered" (Hebrews 5:8), this family's suffering had taught them a great lesson.

Every prayer is not answered as we would like it to be. There have been many families, just as worthy as these two, who, in our mortal eyes, have not had such fortunate answers to their prayers. Still, many of them realize they have received blessings as they have gone through the purification process, no matter the outcome of their prayers. When we prove obedient in adversity we are refined and sanctified in the process.

"Trust in the Lord with All Thine Heart"

"Whatsoever ye ask the Father in my name it shall be given unto you, that is expedient for you" (D&C 88:64). What does "expedient" mean? I believe it means that which is best for us. But only our Father in Heaven knows what will be most beneficial for us. We "see through a glass, darkly" (1 Corinthians 13:12) during our mortal life and do not know what is most desirable for us. Because of our mortal vision it is natural for us to grieve over what we perceive to be unfair. For this reason we are counseled: "Trust in the Lord with all thine heart; and lean not unto thine own understanding" (Proverbs 3:5).

One of our daughters and her husband have been praying to have a child for years. They have gone through painful and expensive tests. They have increased their attention to the Lord's commandments, their attendance at the temple, their study of the scriptures, and their fasting as they pray for a child of their own. Surely theirs is a righteous desire. Still, for now the answer has been in the negative. (For some couples the answer has been "not in this mortal life.") Meantime they have prayed for understanding and peace so that they won't become bitter over their hurt.

It is heartbreaking when people suffer trials but don't learn from them. Some experience pain and, rather than learning obedience and being purified, they become embittered. We need to meet trials in a way that we are lifted by them. When we meet heartache with faith and bear our trials well we will have a special blessing of grace through the Savior's atonement. Jesus suffered not only for our sins but also for our pains, afflictions, and sicknesses (see Alma 7:11–12). The atonement of Jesus Christ can, as Bruce C. Hafen explains, "sweeten all the bitterness we taste"[2] if we do "all we can do" (2 Nephi 25:23) to accept adversity and become purified by it.

"I'm Thankful the Lord Didn't Heal Her"

I know another family who had quite a different experience from the two I have already mentioned. Their first two daughters had normal health, but the third child in their family was severely handicapped with a type of cerebral palsy. In her first year Cindy had been healthy, but then she ceased to develop normally and has been bedfast since that time. She is now eighteen.

When Heather, fifth in the family, was a baby she seemed well until she was about six months old. Then some disturbing symptoms appeared. Can you imagine the parents' anguish when they learned Heather had the same problem as her older sister?

Their sixth child was their first boy and he also seemed active and well, but in a few months his development took a similar course and the doctors again diagnosed the identical disease. To think that three out of six children in one family had such an extreme handicap! The couple and their three healthy children were heartbroken.

The parents chose to keep all of their handicapped children at home. The amount of work their disease caused was monumental; it took the mother six hours a day just to feed them. The story is inspiring but too long to tell here. However, let me tell you one thing the mother expressed. She prayed, "Father, how can I survive having so little sleep?" She reports what happened, "I felt my answer was that perhaps there was something I needed more than sleep." She decided to make a list. Some of the things she put on it were "better home evenings, more scripture study, learn more about Christ and the prophets, live without contention in our home."

Sometimes we think that righteousness will bring relief from trial, but righteousness brings peace, not an easy life. When Heather was eleven years old she died. She had few choices in her life because she was virtually a prisoner in her own body. But in the choices she had been allowed to have, she had made Christlike decisions. She chose to love her family, to be happy, and to love Jesus. Surely she was a most righteous child, yet her heartfelt prayer—just to walk—was never answered affirmatively in all of her eleven years. But her family was blessed by her young life in such marvelous ways that after her death her mother was able to say, "I'm glad a loving Father in Heaven didn't heal Heather when she was six months old and we asked him to."

"We Just Don't Know Why"

When Rex Lee, president of BYU, regained his health after a cruel battle with cancer and was asked why he thought his life was spared, his response was, "We just don't know!" I believe that is true. President Lee said, "The only thing that is really certain is that we just don't know why some people recover from serious illness while others, with the same illness, the same worthiness, and the same faith and prayers, do not."[3]

Whether the answer to our pleadings is in the affirmative or the negative, the path we must take in adversity is clear. We should purify ourselves in all ways possible, pray unceasingly, and work as hard as we can to make the best of the situation.

I know a young woman, Becky Reeve, who was paralyzed after an accident in the mission field. She had to give up many of her dreams —to be the mother of a large family, to be a missionary and teacher —and live on with severe limitations the best she could. Her thoughts demonstrate her great trust in God: "What can I be? I do not like to be average. I like to have goals to work for. I like to be something. Then I decided: I can be a cripple. I do not know how, but I will learn how to be a cripple, and I will be the greatest cripple who has ever lived." The 1989 Relief Society manual adds that "being the greatest cripple for [Becky] includes sharing her faith and encouraging others to trust in the Lord."[4] I have seen her frequently at the temple in her wheelchair, and it is easy to sense her cheerfulness and strong and faithful spirit.

At the funeral of a slain missionary President Gordon B. Hinckley said, "We don't know the purposes of the Lord. We don't know why some things happen."[5] We need to always pray for understanding and acceptance of our trials. We should also seek an eternal perspective and then accept the Lord's will with thanksgiving in *all* things, whether to us they seem to be blessings or trials. "And thou shalt rejoice in every good thing which the Lord thy God hath given unto thee, and unto thine house" (Deuteronomy 26:11).

Elder Russell M. Nelson has taught, "The precise challenge you regard now as 'impossible' may be the very refinement you need, in His eye. . . . With celestial sight, trials impossible to change become possible to endure."[6] If we learn to purify ourselves as we pray for answers and to receive all things with thankfulness, then "after much tribulation come the blessings" (D&C 58:4). In the end we may win the prize of eternal life, and then our longed for earthly desires will be replaced with greater rewards—eternal rewards!

19

Lovingkindness

Lovingkindness, written as one word, is found in the Old Testament some thirty times. David often uses it in his psalms to describe the Lord. In modern scripture it is not found as a single word; rather it is written as two words. Writing it as one word in the old form, however, appeals to me. Lovingkindness is a quality of divinity we must gain to claim the promise of celestial life. For years I have delighted in the sound and thought of this word. How could one word be more symbolic of a Christlike quality than the expression *lovingkindness?* Say it aloud, contemplate it, and I think it will become a favorite of yours too. Its meaning is worth pondering.

I recently attended the funeral of a good friend of mine who lived on the same street we do. A woman in her fifties, she had fought against cancer for well over a decade. During all that time she had not allowed the disease to stop her from striving to become a better person. Her name was Leah. At the viewing we saw her husband and her five grown children and their companions standing by her open casket. As we stood in line to talk to them I thought how truly these children honored their father and mother. They had been taught well, and they had learned and lived their parents' precepts.

Leah was not a college graduate or a community leader; she was something finer. Gracious and compassionate, a student of the scriptures, and a fine instructor of any age group, she was by example and teaching a molder of youth. Her Primary class loved her and wept that she had gone. One of our daughters had her as her Laurel teacher; Leah became a person she wanted to emulate. We were grateful to have our teenager choose Leah as a model during the years when every girl needs an ideal.

A few years ago the bishop called her to be Relief Society president; that same week she learned that her cancer had come back. Some women might have asked to be released, but Leah chose to remain. Every Sunday we saw her smiling. We knew that part of her week, after her treatment, had been spent in bed, but Sundays she was up again and ready to serve us. All of her hair fell out, making it necessary for her to wear a wig. When her hair started to come back, though it was short it was soft, and she looked beautiful to us and inspired us with her leadership.

At the funeral service there was a building full of people; every life there had been influenced by hers. How did she do it? In a tribute to Leah her daughter characterized her well by quoting from the book of Moroni: "But charity is the pure love of Christ, and it endureth forever; and whoso is found possessed of it at the last day, it shall be well with him" (Moroni 7:47).

I'm sure one reason why Leah had an impact on the lives of so many people was that she loved them with this pure love of Christ. I believe this pure quality is what is called in the Old Testament lovingkindness.

Selfishness, the Opposite of Lovingkindness

Recently I finished reading a book. There were three main characters in it. Their interests focused on clothes, travel, luxuriant living accommodations, elegant food, and plenty of fun and recreation. During the course of the book they never cultivated any other interests. Their lives were erratic and they suffered, sometimes because of poverty and sometimes because of wealth, but they didn't learn from their suffering.

Their lives ended and they were as selfish as they had been all along. They never spent time or effort on anyone but themselves. Consequently they didn't love anyone except themselves. When they came to the finale of life they were still seeking for beautiful clothes, travel, luxuriant living accommodations, elegant food, and plenty of fun and recreation. It was rather a dreary story, but very thought-provoking.

The reason why the account was motivating was that the three characters so graphically portrayed the exact opposite of the qualities represented by lovingkindness. We know that embodied in loving-kindness is selflessness. Each of us will be required to develop Christlike love. Indeed, being possessed of it is a requirement for exaltation.

A Family Created through Lovingkindness

There is a couple whose story is touching and tender. They have been married about seventeen years. They are named Steve and Kathy. When Steve was young he always showed empathy for any boy who had been picked on or teased—he reached out to him and made him feel a part of the group by accepting him and standing up for him. Kathy too showed very early in life what a warm heart she had; she cared for those who suffered; she brought home and took care of crippled animals; and she had a special tenderness for children who were mistreated.

This young couple learned soon after they married that they were unlikely to have children of their own. So they adopted a child when they had been married only six months. Subsequently they did have born to them a son and a daughter. However, after these two children came Steve and Kathy were told that there would be no more natural children for them. They knew that adoption of normal children, with three already, was most unlikely.

They began to consider accepting exceptional or handicapped children into their family. Eventually they adopted five more children—four with Down's syndrome and one who was paralyzed. You can imagine that it was all they could do to keep up with their children's tremendous needs—both physical and financial. A few years after the adoption of their last child, Steve and Kathy, with the help of their extended family, were able to arrange for the temple sealing of all of these children to them.

Of course the three older children, now all teenagers, were to be part of this significant event. One Thursday morning in February all ten of them came to the temple. The handicapped children needed a lot of help, and the older children provided it. The couple dressed in white and went to the sealing room. When all was in readiness the eight children were brought to the door; the workers and teenagers assisted the younger children. The door opened and into the room and to the altar came the children, all dressed in white.

When the whole family was gathered at that altar there was not a dry eye in the room. It was a beautiful sight and the consummation of the hope this couple had extended to their children—the sacrifices they had made, the training they had provided, but most especially the selfless love they had felt and exhibited. In the warmth of that love these children will be able to reach their greatest potential, which I feel will be to influence others to practice more love and better live the second great commandment. Surely those who participated in or witnessed that sealing caught an inspiring glimpse of celestial love.

Cultivate Selflessness

What can we do to be filled with this love? Let us decide just how we may help it take root, blossom, and bear fruit in our own characters. One way is to cultivate unselfishness.

One day when one of the sister temple workers was coming into the temple carrying her freshly laundered temple dress, some muddy water was splashed on it, making it impossible for her to wear the dress. When she got to her locker some of the workers from the earlier shift were also dressing, and one of them noticed the soiled dress. She immediately offered one of her own dresses to this sister, who gratefully accepted. They didn't even know each others' names. The next week the borrowed dress was returned with a note of thanks, and a lovely handkerchief with a hand-crocheted edge around it was in the pocket. These two women are fast friends because of an act of unselfishness.

Sharing time or goods, even when we have little of either, sharpens our capacity to feel love. Mother Teresa tells of taking some rice to a Hindu family with eight children. She says their eyes were bright with hunger. While she was still there the mother, before preparing the rice for the family, divided the food, excused herself, and went out. Mother Teresa waited until the woman returned, then asked, "Where did you go? What did you do?" The answer was simple, "They are hungry also." The nun learned that the mother had taken part of the much-needed rice to a Muslim family who lived in similar squalor nearby.[1]

Practice Lovingkindness

Perhaps lovingkindness does not come easily or naturally to us, but practice will make it a part of our personalities. I know you are busy; your time is probably filled almost to capacity. But we do not have to look far for opportunities.

We can find them close to us, and this enables us to practice lovingkindness often. In an average ward there are fifteen people who have chronic mental illness and behavior disorders, six who have communication disorders, ten who have learning disabilities, four who have hearing impairments, two who have visual impairments, and several others who are handicapped in various ways.[2] All around us are those who need acceptance and support. A father said of his nineteen-year-old handicapped daughter, "We love her so; it breaks our hearts to see how she has had to grow up without friends." You can develop lovingkindness just by being friendly to those who are different.

When you want to help someone, don't think that you must take them something you've made. Just take yourself and listen to them when you visit. It is the best gift you can give and doesn't take a great deal of time. When one of our daughters, who lives in Arizona, was a Relief Society president, she and her husband had five children, from age six to seventeen. During the years she served she was unable to spend time with her children in some of the ways she formerly had. Instead she involved them in the compassionate service that came with her calling.

At Christmastime we went with her family to visit residents of a nearby nursing home. I could tell that her husband and children knew many of the people who were there. They had fed them or sung to them or read to them. Even six-year-old Logan, when he went up to each patient, joked with them or held their hands as he talked to them. In those years unselfishness became firmly rooted in the minds of these children, and it grew into a lifelong companion which will always bless them.

All around us there are other opportunities to help in small ways that are not beyond our abilities, time, or strength. Just try smiling, for instance. Smile at the boy who carries out your groceries; smile at the small child who knocks on your door; smile and speak to the elderly person who is so often ignored. If you do this you may come to love these people. In time we may learn to love everyone.

"Wherefore, my beloved brethren, pray unto the Father with all the energy of heart, that ye may be filled with this love, which he hath bestowed upon all who are true followers of his Son, Jesus Christ; . . . that we may have this hope; that we may be purified even as he is pure" (Moroni 7:48). One final way we can seek to have lovingkindness is to make this plea in prayer. Our prayers that we be filled with lovingkindness must be fervent and heartfelt. If we so pray, we will be ready to make our final report when the time arrives, as it did for my friend Leah, for we will be possessed of charity. Then it shall be well with us.

Notes

Introduction: The Diversity of Women and Their Frustrations

1. President Joseph Fielding Smith used similar language to describe the principles found in section 4 of the Doctrine and Covenants. See Daniel H. Ludlow, *A Companion to Your Study of the Doctrine and Covenants*, 2 vols. (Salt Lake City: Deseret Book Co., 1978), 1:66.

Chapter 1. Keep a Cheerful Attitude

1. Jenkin Lloyd Jones, as quoted in Gordon B. Hinckley, *Cornerstones of a Happy Home* [pamphlet] (Salt Lake City: The Church of Jesus Christ of Latter-day Saints, 1984), p. 4.

2. Caroline Eyring Miner, "Joys in Growing Older," in *Joy* (Salt Lake City: Deseret Book Co., 1980), p. 109.

3. Miner, "Joys in Growing Older," p. 109.

Chapter 2. Set Priorities and Simplify, Simplify!

1. Anne G. Osborn (quoting Bruce C. Hafen), "Balance: The Joy of Perspective," in *Joy* (Salt Lake City: Deseret Book Co., 1980), p. 43.

2. Osborn, "Balance," p. 44.

3. Osborn, "Balance," p. 48.

4. Spencer Johnson, *One Minute Mother* (New York: Wm. Morrow Co., 1983).

5. Dallin H. Oaks, "Family History: 'In Wisdom and Order,' " *Ensign* 19 (June 1989): 6, 7.

Chapter 3. Take Time for a Halcyon Day

1. Told by Nadine Matis at a Lion House luncheon, 2 March 1983.

2. *Halcyon* is a beautiful word, not to be confused with Halcion, the sleeping medication.

3. See a similar list in Jo Ann Larsen, "Rattled Nerves, Ragged Egos Demand a Rest from Stress," *Deseret News*, 15 April 1990, sec. S, p. 7.

Chapter 4. Value Yourself

1. See some similar examples in Eileen Gibbons Kump, "The Bread and Milk of Living," in *A Woman's Choices* (Salt Lake City: Deseret Book Co., 1984), pp. 105-6.

2. Russell M. Nelson, "Woman—Of Infinite Worth," *Ensign* 19 (November 1989): 22.

Chapter 5. How Vital Is Communication?

1. Stuart Cooke, "Glad You Asked," *Reader's Digest*, December 1988, p. 93.

2. Carolyn J. Rasmus, "Happiness—the Lord's Way," *Ensign* 18 (March 1988): 48.

3. Russell M. Nelson, *The Power within Us* (Salt Lake City: Deseret Book Co., 1988), p. 32.

Chapter 6. Self-Image and Communication

1. Colette Dowling, quoted in Susan Lyman-Whitney, "Author Chronicles Struggle to Love, Accept Her 'Self,' " *Deseret News*, 12 March 1990, sec. C, p. 3.

2. Quote found in Jo Ann Larsen, "Scales Reveal Your Weight, Not Your Worth," *Deseret News*, 11 February 1990, sec. S, p. 8.

3. See "Helper's High: Volunteering Is Probably Good for Your Health," *Psychology Today*, October 1988.

4. *History of the Church* 4:605.

5. *History of the Church* 4:605.

Chapter 7. Between Husband and Wife

1. Larry Hof and William Miller, quoted in Brent Barlow's marriage column, *Deseret News*, 12 April 1990, sec. C, p. 2.

2. Barlow, marriage column, p. 2.

3. Carlfred Broderick, *Couples* (New York: Simon and Schuster, 1979), pp. 72–73.

4. Term used by Kathleen M. Galvin and Bernard J. Brommel, *Family Communication: Cohesion and Change* (Glenview, Ill.: Scott, Foresman and Company, 1982), p. 58.

5. Virginia Satir, quoted in Galvin and Brommel, *Family Communication*, p. 58.

6. Irene Vogel, quoted in Diane Hales, "Ten Ways to Improve Your Marriage," *McCall's*, July 1986, p. 60.

7. See Samuel A. Schreiner, Jr., "One Question That Can Save a Marriage," *Reader's Digest*, February 1990, pp. 140–42.

8. Bruce C. Hafen, *The Broken Heart* (Salt Lake City: Deseret Book Co., 1989), p. 49.

Chapter 8. Communicating with Children

1. William G. Dyer, *The Sensitive Manipulator* (Provo, Utah: Brigham Young University Press, 1972), pp. 13–14.

2. Murray Straus, "Spanking Kids Can Lead to Violent Behavior," *Deseret News*, 14 May 1990, sec. C, p. 3.

3. See Haim G. Ginott, *Between Parent and Teenager* (New York: Avon Books, 1969), p. 98.

4. H. Burke Peterson, "Preparing the Heart," *Ensign* 20 (May 1990): 83–84.

5. H. Burke Peterson, "Unrighteous Dominion," *Ensign* 19 (July 1989): 8.

6. Glen Latham, quoted in Brent Israelsen, "Be Careful with Words, Educator Tells Adults," *Deseret News*, 2 April 1990, sec. B, p. 1.

7. Robert M. Bramson, quoted in Antonia van der Meer, "A Better Way to Talk to Children," *Reader's Digest*, February 1990, p. 60.

8. Van der Meer, "Better Way," p. 60.

9. See Dyer, *Sensitive Manipulator*, p. 47.

10. The manual for this course is available at LDS Social Services.

Chapter 9. Talking with Teens

1. William G. Dyer, *The Sensitive Manipulator* (Provo, Utah: Brigham Young University Press, 1972), pp. 37–38.

2. See Dyer, *Sensitive Manipulator*, p. 38.

3. See Dyer, *Sensitive Manipulator*, p. 32.

4. Haim G. Ginott, *Between Parent and Teenager* (New York: Avon Books, 1969), p. 82.

5. See *Becoming a Better Parent* [manual] (Salt Lake City: The Church of Jesus Christ of Latter-day Saints, LDS Social Services, 1974), chap. 2, pp. 1–2.

6. Quoted in Ginott, *Parent and Teenager*, pp. 68–69.

7. H. Burke Peterson, "Preparing the Heart," *Ensign* 20 (May 1990): 83–84.

8. Chris Crowe, "How to Talk to Your Parents," *New Era* 19 (February 1989): 14–15.

9. Ginott, *Parent and Teenager*, p. 99.

10. Victor B. Cline, "Ten Keys to Rearing Successful Children," War- ren Report (published in Davis County, Utah, by Tracy Crowell), Winter 1986 issue, p. 20.

11. Howard W. Hunter, "Parents' Concern for Children," *Ensign* 13 (November 1983): 65.

Chapter 10. "Listen with Your Heart!"

1. Quoted in Haim G. Ginott, *Between Parent and Teenager* (New York: Avon Books, 1969), p. 42.

2. William V. Pietsch, quoted in Joseph A. DeVito, *Human Communica- tion: The Basic Course*, 3d ed. (New York: Harper and Row, 1985), p. 64.

3. Quote found in Kathleen M. Galvin and Bernard J. Brommel, *Family Communication: Cohesion and Change* (Glenview, Ill.: Scott, Foresman and Company, 1982), p. 121.

4. DeVito, *Human Communication*, p. 62.

5. See Marion F. Stonberg, *Listen with Your Heart* [pamphlet] (Ameri- can Cancer Society, 1978).

6. See Stonberg, *Listen with Your Heart*.

Chapter 11. You and Aging Parents

1. Russell M. Nelson, "Addiction or Freedom," *Ensign* 18 (November 1988): 7.

2. See Evelyn T. Marshall, "The Widows,' 'Might,' " *Ensign* 18 (March 1988): 52.

Chapter 12. About Unrighteous Dominion

1. Quoted in H. Burke Peterson, "Unrighteous Dominion," *Ensign* 19 (July 1989): 7.

Chapter 13. Friendships with Other Women

1. Joseph A. DeVito, *Human Communication: The Basic Course*, 3d ed. (New York: Harper and Row, 1985), p. 36.

2. Thomas Hughes, in *Elbert Hubbard's Scrapbook* (New York: Wm. H. Wise and Co., 1923), p. 75.

3. Sydney Smith, in *The New Dictionary of Thoughts*, ed. C. N. Catrevas, Jonathan Edwards, and Ralph Emerson Browns (New York: Doubleday and Co., n.d.), p. 224.

Chapter 14. Intimacy in Relationships

1. Victor L. Brown, Jr., *Human Intimacy* (Salt Lake City: Parliament Publishers, 1981), p. 136.

2. Brown, *Human Intimacy*, p. xiv.

3. Spencer W. Kimball, *Marriage* (Salt Lake City: Deseret Book Co., 1978), p. 47.

4. George and Nena O'Neill, quoted in Kathleen M. Galvin and Bernard J. Brommel, *Family Communication: Cohesion and Change* (Glenview, Ill.: Scott, Foresman and Company, 1982), p. 94.

5. William W. Wilmot, *Dyadic Communication*, 2d ed. (Reading, Mass: Addison-Wesley Publishing Co., 1979), p. 71.

6. Rudolph F. Verderber, *Communicate* (Belmont, Calif.: Wadsworth Publishing Co., 1984), p. 93.

7. Brown, *Human Intimacy*, p. 40.

8. Quoted in Galvin and Brommel, *Family Communication*, p. 85.

9. George Eliot, quoted in Charles Wallis, *The Treasure Chest* (New York: Harper and Row, 1965), p. 102.

Chapter 15. Prepare Your Heart

1. *Hymns*, 1948, no. 252.

2. See Thomas S. Monson, *Live the Good Life* (Salt Lake City: Deseret Book Co., 1988), p. 30.

Chapter 16. Gratitude

1. Truman G. Madsen, *Joseph Smith the Prophet* (Salt Lake City: Bookcraft, 1989), p. 104.

2. Spencer W. Kimball, *The Teachings of Spencer W. Kimball* (Salt Lake City: Bookcraft, 1982), p. 233.

3. Quoted in Spencer W. Kimball, *Tragedy or Destiny?* [booklet] (Salt Lake City: Deseret Book Co., 1977), p. 4.

4. See Corrie ten Boom, with John and Elizabeth Sherrill, *The Hiding Place* (Old Tappan, N. J.: Bantam Books, 1971), pp. 197–200.

5. B. Y. Williams, "Your House of Happiness," in *Masterpieces of Religious Verse*, ed. James Dalton Morris (New York: Harper and Row, 1948), p. 305.

Chapter 17. Criticism Is Futile; Judgment Is Crippling

1. N. Eldon Tanner, " 'Judge Not, That Ye Be Not Judged,' " *Ensign* 2 (July 1972): 35.

2. John Prussing, quoted in *Reader's Digest*, December 1988, p. 131.

3. See John H. Groberg, "Writing Your Personal and Family History," *Ensign* 10 (May 1980): 49.

4. Edwin Markham, in *Richard Evans' Quote Book* (Salt Lake City: Publishers Press, 1971), p. 181.

5. Spencer W. Kimball, *The Miracle of Forgiveness* (Salt Lake City: Bookcraft, 1969), p. 267.

Chapter 18. In Adversity, Purify and Pray

1. See Spencer W. Kimball, *The Teachings of Spencer W. Kimball* (Salt Lake City: Bookcraft, 1982), pp. 167–68.

2. Bruce C. Hafen, *The Broken Heart* (Salt Lake City: Deseret Book Co., 1989), p. 29.

3. Rex E. Lee and Janet Lee, "Beauty in the Storm," BYU Winter Devotional, 23 January 1990, typescript, p. 14.

4. See "Unfulfilled Expectations," *Relief Society Personal Study Guide 1989* (Salt Lake City: The Church of Jesus Christ of Latter-day Saints, 1988), p. 287.

5. Gordon B. Hinckley, quoted in *Church News*, 9 June 1990, p. 3.

6. Russell M. Nelson, " 'With God Nothing Shall Be Impossible,' " *Ensign* 18 (May 1988): 35.

Chapter 19. Lovingkindness

1. See Vaughn J. Featherstone, *The Disciple of Christ* (Salt Lake City: Deseret Book Co., 1984), p. 37.

2. See Carmen B. Pingree, "Six Myths about the Handicapped," *Ensign* 18 (June 1988): 20.

Index